Ron Rubin is the Minister of Tea and the Chairman of the Board for The Republic of Tea, one of the most successful and fastest-growing cachet brands in America today. He is also the co-author of the highly acclaimed Zentrepreneur Guides series, including *Success At Life—How to Catch and Live Your Dream* and *Dragon Spirit—How to Self-Market Your Dream* (Newmarket Press).

John-Michael photo

Michael McMyne, a student at Spring Hill College, is one of the nation's youngest motivational speakers. He travels the country challenging audiences to rise to the challenges of life. Michael has toppled many barriers in his own life. After being diagnosed with Chronic Obstructive Pulmonary Disorder, Attention Deficit Hyperactivity Disorder, and dyslexia, he decided not only to become well, but also to excel. Since then he has gained national acclaim as a speaker and author. His first book, *Real Life University*, was published in 2001. He is the President and CEO of McMyne & Associates, LLC, and in 2002 he was named the Global Student Entrepreneur for Social Impact by the Global Student Entrepreneur Awards program.

STUDENT ENTREPRENEURS

14 Undergraduate All-Stars Tell Their Stories

COMPILED BY **MICHAEL McMYNE**
EDITED BY **NICOLE AMARE** PhD

*Student Entrepreneurs: 14 Undergraduate
All-Stars Tell Their Stories*

Compiled by Michael McMyne
Edited by Nicole Amare

Published by PREMIUM PRESS AMERICA

ISBN 1-887654-15-1
Library of Congress Catalog Number: 2003109704

Design by Armour&Armour

First Edition 2003
1 2 3 4 5 6 7 8 9 10

We dedicate this book to
Sharon Bower
whose love, patience, and dedication
have made each of us Superstars

Contents

Foreword

It is with true pleasure that I am able to help bring this book into being. The stories contained herein offer a ringside seat, a close-up view of youthful energetic doers who were compelled to act on their visions, hopes and dreams. These stories are told by young college "undergraduate" entrepreneurs themselves, who understand that the future is not something that you wait for to happen, but rather it is something that you can create and make happen.

Acting on their passion, choosing to travel the road of possibility, these entrepreneurs share their journeys of success and fulfillment, showing us all that whatever it is you choose to do or be isn't a matter of start-up capital; it is instead, simply, a matter of making the choice to start to make the commitment to live the life that you know is yours. Each of these stories is a case study in itself, allowing us to bear witness to the passion and perseverance that is necessary to turn a dream into a reality. More importantly, their experiences hold a light to the fact that for the entrepreneur, no greater business plan exists than the plan that you have for yourself.

—Ron Rubin

Ron Rubin is the Minister of Tea and the Chairman of the Board for The Republic of Tea, one of the most successful and fastest-growing cachet brands in America today. He is also the co-author of the highly acclaimed Zentrepreneur Guides series, including Success At Life— How to Catch and Live Your Dream *and* Dragon Spirit—How to Self-Market Your Dream *(Newmarket Press).*

Preface

Entrepreneurship has a long and storied history in our culture. Millions of people all around the globe have taken the leap of faith to start and run their own business. These successful, thirsty people have the drive, dedication, and desire to make their ventures both profitable and enjoyable. Who are these people and what exactly is their motivation? More importantly, where do they get the know-how to begin the daunting task of starting a business?

This book will introduce you to fourteen amazing college students who serve as living examples that entrepreneurship is for anyone and everyone. The stories you read will take you through the trials and tribulations of the globe's most recognized college entrepreneur all-stars. Most importantly, however, this manuscript will introduce to you real stories of success attained by hard work, dedication, and an unyielding commitment to a dream.

As the executive director and founder of the Global Student Entrepreneur Awards program, Sharon Bower has worked arduously to ensure that the go-getters in college who manage both a profitable business and a full course load should be recognized. Ms. Bower's vision has allowed winners throughout the globe to grow their businesses through the prestigious Global Student Entrepreneur[SM] Awards program. Ms. Bower's circle of support extends far beyond the sponsors that allow the program to exist—ultimately, without Saint Louis University, this program would not continue to thrive.

Just six short months ago, the CEO of one of America's most thriving companies, The Republic of Tea, made the decision that the stories of each Global Student Entrepreneur[SM] Awards winner were so powerful and compelling that people all over the world should have the opportunity to read and benefit from them. Ron Rubin not only brought this book into existence but has breathed life into it from its conception. He is a true example of what a successful entrepreneur really is—Mr. Rubin is not only a successful businessman, but he is also a humanitarian and a philanthropist who is dedicated to the continual growth of entrepreneurship across the globe.

The president of Spring Hill College, the Reverend Greg Lucy, SJ, opened my freshman year of college by warning me and my classmates of the shipwrecks that we would encounter along our journey. His words of inspiration aided me in my matriculation at Spring Hill College; moreover, the warning of shipwrecks helped me in my entrepreneurial endeavors. His warning prepared me for the realization that every sea is not calm. Indeed, I have encountered numerous shipwrecks while in college—some related to academics and others to business. However, those shipwrecks did not discourage my progress, but rather they guided my growth.

This book is filled with stories of shipwrecks. This book is also filled with stories not only of individuals who survived those shipwrecks but also of those entrepreneurs who actually went on to use these disastrous situations to their advantage. These fourteen entrepreneurs will demonstrate to you through their personal anecdotes and words of wisdom that even the best entrepreneurs make mistakes and fail, but the ones who remain successful do so because they never give up. Good entrepreneurs all know that the storm of disaster eventually passes. Great entrepreneurs know when it's time to abandon ship altogether and either swim on their own or seek out a new ship.

I invite you to take all you can from the following pages. Learn from these entrepreneurs about what to do when starting your business and more importantly what not to do. Listen to them when they show you that the best businesses are formed out of an existing hobby, something with which you already enjoy and have expertise. Believe them when not just one author or two but all of them tell you to write a business plan first; without one, you'll make the road to success that much longer and harder. Finally, use their advice and make a difference in the world. Who knows? You could very well be the next winner of the Global Student Entrepreneur[SM] Awards. Good luck and anchors aweigh!

—Michael McMyne

Acknowledgments

As the compiler of this book, I have come in contact with so many incredible people who have helped make this project a reality that they deserve special recognition:

First, to the brilliant and magnificent Sharon Bower, your vision and energy have made each Global Student Entrepreneur Award winner a real Superstar;

To Ron Rubin, for graciously opening the door to making this book a reality and for taking the project from zero to sixty in no time flat! Your guidance and experience helped me in more ways than you can ever know;

To Leah Kruger and Jeanne Rhodes, your hard work and dedication allowed this project to run smoothly;

To our editor, Nicole Amare, Ph.D., for working arduously to comply with our demanding deadlines and for your wisdom that helped guide this project. Thanks, friend.

To Francis Bologna, whose backyard is the greatest think tank on the planet. Your encouragement is what started this whole writing revolution;

To Mike McCrossen, for your guidance and vision. No words can ever express my gratitude;

To the amazingly creative Greg Buisson, your generosity and wisdom put this book in the hands of our readers, you are the real all-star;

To Todd Murphy, your connections have truly helped plug me in;

To the professional team that guides my company—Leo Kern and Albert Nicaud—thank you from the bottom of my heart;

To the faculty and staff at St. Catherine of Siena School, for your constant encouragement;

To Irvin Barousse, for believing in me when no one else did;

To the faculty and staff at Spring Hill College, for nurturing me in body, mind, and spirit. A special thank you to Patricia Mark, Ph.D., you always find a ray of light in any situation;

To the entire Communication Arts Department at Spring Hill—faculty, staff, and friends alike—thank you for your wisdom, guidance, and support;

To all of my friends on the Hill, especially Neil Hatchard, for your unfailing friendship and encouragement;

To my roommates, Neil, Dom, and Andy, thank you for your constant support;

To John Thomas, for your 3:00 A.M. pep-talks and your willingness to do anything to help;

To Gayel Richardson, you are an A+ teacher;

To the Dublikar family, thank you for your support, encouragement, and friendship;

To LeeMarie Martinez, for being my pillar of support, I love you;

And finally, to my family, thank you for encouraging me to dream big.

—Michael McMyne

Beyond the Lemonade Stand . . .

Tales from Undergraduate Business Owners

Once upon a time there was a lemonade stand. . . .
Many times on warm St. Louis summer afternoons and evenings, I have driven through my neighborhood, passing two or three kids hawking a cool drink from behind their lemonade stand—beacons of our American free enterprise system. These nascent childhood businesses are launched with assistance from the home front—a table and tablecloth provided by Mom and Dad (or better yet, a quickly assembled booth made of cast-off lumber), some lemonade from the kitchen pantry, a pitcher and paper cups, and a shoebox holding spare change from the piggy bank. The future springs from these adventures of childhood, and I am struck by the many times I hear our winners tell of their youthful experiences of entrepreneurship, many of them including those legendary lemonade stands.

When that first neighborhood customer stops and purchases a cool drink, the budding entrepreneur receives positive reinforcement. The Global Student Entrepreneur℠ Awards were designed to continue that reinforcement by spotlighting the best businesses run by undergraduates.

I was able to develop the Global Student Entrepreneur℠ Awards because of the support of Saint Louis University, which in 1987 established the Jefferson Smurfit Center for Entrepreneurial Studies in the John Cook School of Business. Since that time, the center has gone on to win numerous national awards and accolades under the leadership of the Center's director and Coleman Chair in Entrepreneurship, Robert H. Brockhaus. Saint Louis University has a long tradition of producing outstanding entrepreneurs who, in the Jesuit tradition, have given back generously to their alma mater and their community. In this supportive atmosphere, the awards were first "birthed" in 1988 and offered only to students in the state of Missouri. In 1997, the program was expanded beyond Missouri's borders. After spreading throughout North America to include Mexico, Canada, the Caribbean, and all fifty states, the 2003 program now includes Australia and New Zealand as well. Further international expansion is anticipated as more and more countries want the experience of global competition for their students.

The two-tiered Global Awards begin at the regional level where students compete against others from their region. The regions vary in size from as small as several states to as large as an entire country, like Canada or Mexico. Each region is administered by a regional partner/director at a school or organization devoted to entrepreneurship. These partners are a creative lot, innovative in promoting the awards and building awareness, and a major component in the success of the program. In addition, their institutions put a priority on entrepreneurship, as evidenced by their involvement. Each region sends their first-place winner to compete for the top Global Awards.

Our goal for the Global Student Entrepreneur℠ Awards is to become the premier award for undergraduate entrepreneurs. We believe that by spreading the experiences of the winners to new audiences through this book, we will accelerate the pace of achieving our goal. These winners set an example of positive ethical economic activity. For young people around the world who aspire to control their own destiny, there are lessons to be learned in these pages. For young people around the world who need hope and a model to pattern after, there are examples in these pages to choose from. Our winners' successes and setbacks will enlighten the next generation.

The Global Student Entrepreneur℠ Awards attempt to uncover all those students who are trying to balance payrolls and papers, checkbooks and classes, taxes and tests. We want to let the rest of the world know of their accomplishments. The current fact is that no one really knows the true extent of student entrepreneurship on university and college campuses. We do know this much: Entrepreneurship is being taught at more and more schools; entrepreneurship centers and endowed chairs outstrip the ability to fill them with professors, teachers, and business leaders; the media grab stories of young entrepreneurs as fast as they learn of them; websites with information and stories of successful young entrepreneurs are springing up; entrepreneurship clubs abound—and all of this has occurred with an accelerating pace during the past twenty years.

My job as creator and director of the awards is exciting and FUN! The best part is interacting with the winning student entrepreneurs. What an incredible bunch they are. You will not be able to read this book without being inspired by their bold innovativeness and their determination.

This book became a reality because of one such winner, Michael McMyne, plus another remarkable individual, Ron Rubin. At the 2002 Awards in Washington, D.C., Michael came to me and said he wanted to discuss an idea, then presented the project—a book that would include all the winners as authors. I had an immediate positive response to this exciting idea and pledged my support. Subsequently, Michael and I began looking for funding for the book. Into this scenario walked Ron Rubin, owner of a highly successful company, The Republic of Tea, and a published author. He immediately saw the book's potential to inspire others and pledged the financial support needed. Without these two, this book would have remained unwritten. They are the sparks that have fanned a brush fire. And, with the promise of publication of two additional editions to be written by future winners, the fire will continue to spread.

Individually, who are these remarkable student entrepreneurs? The winners of the Global Student Entrepreneur[SM] Awards for the past two years have an average age of 22½. Most are juniors and seniors (with a few sophomores), and they come from large universities, small liberal arts schools, technical and art schools, and community colleges. They attend private and public institutions. In other words, they are all around us!

Their businesses run the gamut from high tech to low tech, manufacturing to service. Some of their markets are limited to the population on campus, while the markets of others are international. Some have partners; others go it alone. But in one aspect, they are all similar—they face stiff obstacles when they try to obtain financing through traditional lending institutions. Age and lack of assets are against them. So, most rely on family, friends, and whatever credit cards they can max out. But persevere they do! In 2002, the combined sales of the contributing authors was over $1.2 million dollars, and they had over sixty-five employees. Despite hindrances, they are running solid businesses with enormous potential for future growth.

The winners are not only concerned with running their business but also with their communities and the world around them. One employs disabled workers, while others offer employment opportunities and training for unemployed and underemployed workers. Others donate their products to local charities for auction. One serves as a U.S. representative for the Youth Employment Summit. One helps save coral reefs through her business. Another provides internships for area students. One donates two computer systems to impoverished families at Christmas. One campus business gives back to its student government for distribution to student groups working in the community. One cleans up local lakes while collecting materials for his business. Organizations and efforts that have benefited from their time and contributions include: Canadian inner-city hockey leagues, National Foundation for Teaching Entrepreneurship, terminally ill children, Cystic Fibrosis Foundation, National Coalition for Empowering Young Entrepreneurs, Handicapped Children Sports Activity, and the Special Olympics. One company allows its customers to decide which nonprofits will receive fifteen percent of the company's yearly profits. And finally, one sponsors rehabilitation of basketball facilities in two public schools. Quite a list!

These winners are a resilient lot, and their stories are meant to inspire all who read them. We hear many times that aspiring entrepreneurs want to learn from other successful entrepreneurs who are in their own age bracket. Thus, this book was a natural extension of the Global Student Entrepreneur^SM Awards. We are certain that when this book gets into the hands of enough college students, high school kids, and even middle and elementary school students, it will have an impact.

David Kirby is a noted entrepreneurship professor at the University of Surrey in the United Kingdom and author of *Entrepreneurship*, a book devoted to theory and the application of theory to practice. He states, ". . . we ought to develop entrepreneurial know how and skills in our young people if we are to succeed in a rapidly changing and uncertain world, as entrepreneurs are people who can not only cope with change but can initiate it." David, you will be happy to know that we are attempting to do just that.

José Romaguera, director of the awards program for the Caribbean, says, "Of all the initiatives I have been involved in during my academic career (including when I was dean of the University of Puerto Rico/Mayaguez Business School, where I continue as a professor in the area of entrepreneurship), this is the most significant one in terms of both current and future impact." José is attempting the daunting task of changing the culture of Puerto Rico into an entrepreneurial one. He is doing this by prominently featuring the student entrepreneurs on the front page of newspapers and by showing clips of the winners and their businesses in movie theaters. He is making "superstars" of these outstanding students, positioning them as role models for the youth of the island and is on his way toward making entrepreneurship a viable career option for the youth of Puerto Rico.

Our winners have already had an impressive impact on their individual campuses, their community, and on other students in their immediate areas as they are often asked to share their story and insights with other students. And now, their stories will have an even larger ripple effect. These winners want to give back for the future.

In the short six-year history of the Global Awards, our prior winners have had enormous success. One business has grown into a internationally recognized design firm with over twenty employees; another has distribution for her almonds in over forty states throughout the U.S. with over one million dollars in annual sales and a seventy-five percent annual growth rate; and yet another went on to buy his competitor (expanding his business many times) and was named the Ernst & Young Emerging Entrepreneur, only two years after winning our award. Another winner says, "Winning has truly given me the confidence to step out and try a new venture on a much broader scale."

Our award program would not be possible without the generous support of foundations and corporations. A special thanks go to the following that have supported us through these first six years: The Coleman Foundation, our first foundation sponsor; The Kauffman Center for Entrepreneurial Leadership; The Edward Lowe Foundation; Edward Jones, our first corporate sponsor; Northwestern Mutual Financial Network; and Enterprise Rent-A-Car.

Once upon a time there was a lemonade stand. . . .

Most stories that begin this way end with "and they lived happily ever after." For the winners featured in this book, I wish you happiness ever after and prosperous businesses as well. For you the reader, I wish you inspiration to get moving today toward your entrepreneurial dreams. And the next time you drive or walk past a lemonade stand—STOP! Have a refreshing drink, help an aspiring entrepreneur, and play your part in building a better tomorrow.

—Sharon K. Bower

Sharon K. Bower is creator and director of Global Student Entrepreneur[SM] Awards and associate director of Jefferson Smurfit Center for Entrepreneurial Studies at John Cook School of Business, Saint Louis University.

Turning 25¢ into $1: The Unique Advantages and Disadvantages of Being Young Entrepreneurs

Nick Tostenrude

EnableMart

FIRST PLACE
2002
Global Student
Entrepreneur
Awards

2002 Global Collegiate Entrepreneur
Pacific Northwest Region
Regional Partner: Seattle University

Nick Tostenrude

Nick Tostenrude and Dennis Moulton founded EnableMart after meeting during their freshman year at the University of Portland in Oregon. EnableMart began as a rehabilitation software company based on the research of Moulton's father but soon switched to focus on helping individuals with disabilities. EnableMart began assisting individuals in the search for assistive-technology solutions in the fall of 2001. EnableMart currently sells hundreds of assistive-technology products and enabling devices. Dennis and Nick have grown EnableMart into a multi-million dollar corporation with customers in all fifty states and over twenty foreign countries. In addition to its sales, the company has performed contract work for Microsoft Corporation, Goodwill Industries, and other large organizations to help support Dennis and Nick's mission in the disability industry.

Nick graduated from the University of Portland in the spring of 2002 with a degree in electrical engineering. As a two-year captain of the University of Portland men's tennis team, Nick was awarded All-Conference Doubles and All-Academic honors. Nick also was a member of the University's Entrepreneurial Scholar program, which allowed him to travel to Chile, New York, and California to meet and study successful entrepreneurs. Nick attended Columbia River High School in Vancouver, Washington, and grew up camping, riding dirt bikes, and playing tennis with his two brothers, Joe and Jeff, and his parents, Mike and Marlane.

EnableMart

FOUNDERS: Nick Tostenrude, Dennis Moulton
WEB: enablemart.com
EMAIL: nick@enablemart.com
dennis@enablemart.com
PHONE: 888/640-1999
ADDRESS: 400 Columbia St. Suite 100
Vancouver WA 98660

Turning 25¢ into $1 was easy in elementary school. You could buy and sell some JollyRanchers, make your buck, and go buy some baseball cards. A few years go by and now, instead of turning 25¢ into $1, you want to turn $1 into $2,000,000. This undertaking might seem impossible when you've got $1 in your pocket, but when you're finally at $2,000,000, you will be able to look back and see the pathway from start to finish in a clear, simplified light.

Turning a small amount of resources into a great financial return requires a lot of time, commitment, and hard work. The closest analogy to having your own business is having a child. From the beginning, both require constant nurturing. It is your responsibility to make sure your child stays healthy and grows, just as it is also your responsibility that your business stays healthy and grows. You are preparing your child for success. You are preparing your business for success. These responsibilities are the ultimate test in both parenting and business. When you succeed, you are a thriving entrepreneur and the owner of a solid business.

How and when do you know if you've succeeded? Is it when you hire your first employee? Is it when you make your first profit? Or is it when you sell your company and retire in the Bahamas? The level of success depends on the person. You know better than anyone else who you are, what you consider success, and where you want to take your business. These three things will be your greatest assets during your journey.

Find a Niche

Nine out of ten new businesses fail within the first five years. What's the problem? Why is it so hard to start a successful business? It's difficult to understand why so many businesses never make it ... until you try to do it yourself.

It was the spring of our freshman year when we first

developed the idea to begin a Web-based distributor of as-sistive technology. Soon into the start-up process, we real-ized that there were an endless number of roadblocks that we would need to overcome in order to create a successful com-pany. The challenges of beginning our own business were de-ceitfully overwhelming, especially for young entrepreneurs like us. Although we realized the process of starting a busi-ness in general is difficult, there were a number of additional challenges we faced as young entrepreneurs. Lack of man-agement experience and business associates, the absence of money, and obligations such as school are all obstacles to the young entrepreneur, many of which are often magnified be-cause of youth. However, it eventually became evident that being young entrepreneurs presented many significant bar-riers but ultimately gave us unique advantages that led to the success of our company.

In 1999, we started the **mindnautilus.com** corporation to develop rehabilitative software and Internet-based programs for people who were recovering from traumatic brain injuries. This idea was based on a company that Dennis's father, Gary Moulton, formed back in the days of the first Apple II com-puters. At the time, the available computer technology was not sophisticated enough to support the high-speed and in-tense graphics required to make this software effective. Gary's company proved to be ahead of its time and eventually failed.

We wanted to revitalize this idea and combine it with today's technology to create software and Internet-based pro-grams that increased the cognitive skills of traumatic brain injury patients and other younger learners. We saved the name of the original company, added a *.com* to it, and legally incorporated on March 3, 2000. We had completed the first of the multiple-step process of beginning a business.

Since our incorporation, our company has taken many

unexpected turns. Our original idea wasn't as easy to implement as we first thought. There was serious research, development, programming, and testing that would need to take place. Hundreds of thousands of dollars in capital would be needed, and we were looking at a minimum of three to four years before we had a finished product. We were forced to re-examine our idea and decided to focus specifically on helping people with disabilities access computers. While researching the **mindnautilus.com** corporation, it had become apparent that we had found an unfulfilled niche.

There are over fifty-four million people with disabilities in the United States alone. Many of them need custom products to help them access their computers or assistive technologies. The assistive technology industry seemed to be made up of small, mom-and-pop companies that manufactured one or two products and had little money to market the products. Moreover, a large number of individuals with disabilities had no idea that these products were even offered. We saw this hole between the assistive technology manufacturers and the people who could benefit the most from their products. We decided to focus on filling this gap and connecting the right people with the right technologies. Soon after, we started doing business as EnableMart, exposing niche products to make it easy for people to find exactly what assistive technology they needed.

School vs. Work

Being a student and an entrepreneur was something that we struggled with as we were often faced with questions such as "Do we study for the test tomorrow or work on our business plan?" The one thing we came to realize is that we would have to inevitably end up making quite a few sacrifices in order to concentrate on creating a successful company. There were occasions when the company took precedence over class, sports, socializing, and even sleep. It became impossible trying to balance the two full-time jobs of beginning a company and school. In the end, school was a priority that could not just be put to the side; it had to be completely eliminated for Dennis. He left school to work on the company full time with the intent on finishing later, while Nick continued to try to balance school, work, and being a Division I athlete.

Though school and work often conflicted with each other, it was obvious that the combination was something necessary to ensure the success of our company. Although combining school and starting a business initially seemed like a bad thing, in reality it was a worthwhile experience, one that we have come to value. The choices we made concerning school created advantages that ultimately outweighed the most serious threats to our success. Throughout the start-up process, our youth proved to be something that we could obviously not change but instead use as a tool to facilitate risk-taking. We knew that we had little to lose. If the company failed, we were still young enough to continue an education or begin another company. We had the opportunity to focus on the potential success of the company, not the failure of our lives.

Many older entrepreneurs have a spouse, children, and major assets that they must take into consideration when making business decisions as they can all be enormous losses if the company fails or becomes an overwhelming task. We had none of these things to lose, leaving us with the ability to take major risks and eventually create a successful company.

Creating a Team

It is often said that the most important aspect of a business to an investor is the management team. We repeatedly heard that "investors don't invest in companies; they invest in people!" Fresh out of our teens, we knew that it was unrealistic to expect any investors to take us seriously without a couple of seasoned veterans on our side. We set up a board of advisors and within a couple months, we had a nice group of industry pioneers signed on. The problem was that they were only advisors and none of them was going to take an active role is running the company. We knew we could run the company ourselves. We didn't necessarily want someone else trying to call the shots, but we needed credibility and money, and adding experienced members to our management team would help us achieve these goals.

After some networking at local entrepreneurship events, we found the perfect candidate. We found an older, apparently successful entrepreneur who seemed to have a passion for working with start-ups. We couldn't have asked for a better person to have in our corner. We decided to formalize our relationship with this man, but we had absolutely no experience drafting employment contracts. Naturally, when he suggested that he draft up a "pretty standard agreement that he had used numerous times in the past," we felt like some pressure had been lifted off our backs.

A week later, we met in downtown Portland, Oregon, and he presented a complex contract containing legal clauses that might as well have been written in Japanese. We were a bit thrown back, but this individual seemed trustworthy because, after all, he believed in our idea. So we signed the contract and celebrated hiring our new chairperson. It felt very rewarding to have an experienced businessman believe in your start-up company. It really meant something to us that a man close to triple our age respected what we were starting enough to sign on as our first outside team member.

It didn't take long, however, to learn that we just made a

big mistake. The next couple months seemed to go by quickly and we began to make several advancements with the company. Our new chairman helped us find a financial genius to get our pro-forma financial statements and budgets in order. We figured out how much money we were going to need to raise and we started looking for investors. It was not long, though, before we hit a major roadblock. Our once-active chairman simply stopped doing anything. He went from proactively working with us, to trying to just be our coach, to cutting off total communication.

We soon realized that we had gotten lured into a seemingly interminable contract that lawyers have laughed at on several occasions. It included a nice chunk of stock with a non-dilution clause. There was a put-option allowing him to sell his shares at any time to anybody. His work description was so vague that we could never hold him at fault for sub-par performance. He was entitled to fifteen percent of any capital that the company raised. If we ever raised any money, he was entitled to a nice paycheck or twenty-five percent of the president's salary, whichever was greater. And worst of all, it was signed by us personally, not on behalf of our corporation. Of course, we didn't know that all of this was in the contract until we wanted to fire him. After taking the contract to several lawyers, we found that there was nothing significant we could do other than avoid any actions that would allow him to take advantage of his contract.

We went on, knowing that we would eventually have to deal with the contract. There was no way we could raise the significant amount of money we were originally seeking. No investor would consider a company with this type of contract bearing down on it. Therefore, we decided to grow the company more slowly. We obtained some seed financing by selling stock to our friends and families. This capital got us to the point where we could be a fully operational company. Two years and twenty thousand dollars later, we were able to buy out our chairman and terminate his contract.

We later found out we weren't the only ones who had unpleasant experiences with our former chairman and that it wasn't the first time our lawyer had come across his name. It turned out that we learned a lot from this man. The first lesson he taught us was that not everyone is looking out for your best interests. Being young, we sometimes took this for granted and assumed that everyone was on our side and wanted us to succeed. The second lesson we learned from our former chairman was to read and understand anything you sign as it could mean the failure of your company.

However, the saying "with the bad comes the good" remains partially true in this case. Without running into our chairman, we would have never found our CFO. Without our CFO, we would not have looked credible enough to gain our current CEO, and without a strong board, we would have had a difficult time trying to hire employees who would feel secure in their jobs.

The End Result

After a great deal of trial-and-error, we grew from our experiences and now have the successful company known as EnableMart. Implementing what we knew, learning from mistakes we made, researching, and being motivated and aggressive are just some of the means we used to get us where we are today. Although our young age played a huge role in the problems we faced, we recognized our youth as being an opportunity to bring fresh ideas to the company, take risks, and ultimately achieve our greatest goals. Even now, we realize how lucky we are to have created such a successful company and that obstacles presented because of issues such as age and lack of experience never discouraged our dreams of success-ful venture. And even if EnableMart had never come to be, we know that if our company had failed, at least we would have succeeded at trying.

Dreaming the Impossible Dream

Michael McMyne
McMyne and Associates

Social Impact Award
Southeast Region
Regional Partner:
Kennesaw State University

Michael McMyne

Michael McMyne has dedicated his life to helping the less fortunate by creating the Giving Back Foundation, which has raised hundreds of thousands of dollars for charity. Along with being an accomplished motivational speaker, Michael has published his first book, *Real Life University*; has been awarded the "Key to the City" in Kenner, Louisiana, his hometown; been honored with a "Michael McMyne Day" by New Orleans Mayor Marc Morial for his community service; and been named a "Louisiana Quiet Hero" by CBS affiliate WWL-TV in New Orleans.

JOHN-MICHAEL PHOTO

After receiving life-changing medical care in Denver, Colorado, for the lung disease that plagued his childhood, he founded his company, McMyne & Associates, LLC, a motivational speaking agency. He wrote *Real Life University* when he was 19 years old and a freshman in college. Michael developed his skill of talking well in front of groups into a professional speaking career, becoming one of the nation's youngest recognized speakers ever. Because of the success of his company, he was named the 2002 Global Student Entrepreneur for Social Impact. As a freshman at Spring Hill College in Mobile, Alabama, Michael was awarded the Dean's Leadership Cup, an award given to the freshman student with the most promising leadership potential. Michael is currently completing his senior year at Spring Hill College and is developing software with one of his new companies, Multiple Marketing Associates.

McMyne and Associates

FOUNDER:	Michael McMyne
WEB:	reallifeuniversity.com
EMAIL:	michael@reallifeuniversity.com
PHONE:	504/461-5600
ADDRESS:	3120 Kansas Avenue Kenner LA 70065

The date is September 12, 2002. The time is 7:40 A.M. As I talk on the telephone to a big contributor, my father is loading the truck with hundreds of cases of soda, beer, and food. My mother is meticulously looking over the to-do list that I have prepared. My twin sister is preparing my tuxedo for the evening, and my older twin brothers are on their way to the reception hall to lead the set-up process. I hang up the phone, and out of the corner of my eye, I see my former third grade teacher arrive. A tear is rolling down her cheek. "I'm so proud of you, Michael; you have come such a long way," she says. We hug, and I thank her for coming to help. My phone rings, and I answer. On the other end are my grandparents: "We know you will do just fine tonight. Say a prayer and trust in the Lord like you always have." Fourteen hours later it is over—for the third year in a row, the Giving Back Foundation has raised over forty thousand dollars for terminally ill and underprivileged children.

How did my family and I get to September 12, 2002?

It all started in an unlikely place and in an unlikely manner: a hospital bed, 1,400 miles from my home and with a desperate promise to God. After suffering with Chronic Obstructive Pulmonary Disorder for more than three years, my doctor (with little hope of curing my illness) sent me to National Jewish Hospital in Denver, Colorado, where I would eventually receive the treatment that not only saved my life but also changed it forever. During the second week of my hospital stay, as I cried myself to sleep, I begged and pleaded with God to make me well. I promised Him that if He cured me and helped my brothers through their troubling days as active gang members, I would use my life to help those in need. Three weeks after I arrived in Denver, I went home on some medication to find my brothers waiting for me at the airport so that they could hug me. Until that moment, I could not recall the last time that I got a hug from my brothers. I experienced a miracle, not only a medical miracle but a familial one as well. At that moment, I decided it was my time to start giving back.

Just a short time after I returned home from Denver, I was invited to speak at a national student convention. The organization requested that I make a presentation about overcoming challenges and dealing with the unexpected. It seemed as though I was a perfect fit! I worked for three weeks on that presentation, and I delivered it to an audience of twelve hundred students, who sent me away with a standing ovation. That standing ovation led to a career that would eventually lead to my being named the 2002 Global Student Entrepreneur for Social Impact. Following that first speech, I received more than a dozen calls from schools throughout the country, inviting me to speak to their student body. I graciously accepted their offers and began my first tour as a motivational speaker, but there was one problem . . . I wasn't getting paid. While I thoroughly enjoyed the speaking engagements, it seemed almost unfair that I would spend hundreds of hours preparing, traveling, and delivering the presentations for free. I loved what I was doing, but I also needed to get paid for doing it, so I decided to start my own company. This was the beginning of McMyne & Associates, LLC. In addition to the start of my for-profit company, my dad continued to remind me of my promise that I had made—the promise to give back. A short time after I returned home from the hospital, my first opportunity to give back came. After hearing of a local police officer who was badly burned in a fireworks explosion, I began raising money for his family through a silent auction and dinner/dance. Although I was only seventeen years old at the time, I was able to persuade top civic and business leaders to join in my efforts. Little did I know that we would raise over twenty thousand dollars! That initial opportunity to give back grew into what has become known as The Giving Back Foundation—a 501(c)3, tax-exempt, not-for-profit organization. With the help off my family and numerous volunteers, we have raised more than two hundred fifty thousand dollars for terminally ill and underprivileged children nationwide through this foundation. Not only has the Giving Back Foundation allowed me to help those in need, but it also has helped my family members realize the value of one another.

However, giving back takes more than just a desire to be charitable. As an entrepreneur, you must first become successful so that you have the opportunity to help others. The reward you will receive for working hard to help your community will make you feel like a rare and precious diamond. However, diamonds originally come from coal; it takes years of pressure and heat for a piece of coal to become a diamond. But when a diamond is first discovered, it's often called a "diamond in the rough" because it has not yet been cleaned and polished to resemble the precious stones that we see on many women's third fingers. Young entrepreneurs are very similar in that they start out rough and inexperienced, but with the right steps, entrepreneurs can become rare and valuable community leaders. Most of us know that diamonds are ranked based on four criteria, also called the four "C"s—carat, clarity, color, and cut. In order to be more than just a diamond in the rough, however, entrepreneurs must be prepared to face and act on the five Cs of entrepreneurship: Cost, Customer Service, Change, Charity, and Character.

COST. In order to start your business, figure out how much money you are going to need. One of the best ways to do this is to write up a business plan. (See the "Develop a Plan" paragraph later in this chapter.)

CUSTOMER SERVICE. Most and perhaps all businesses rely on customers to make money. In order to make sure that your customers are happy with what you are doing with your company, ask yourself this simple question: what would I want as a customer? It is also extremely important when you are starting out a business to have constant and effective customer feedback. Give your just-starting business a boost by allowing for this feedback; you'll receive valuable advice about what you're doing right—and wrong. For example, I encourage my audiences to provide comments on my speaking engagements via a handout at the end of my speeches and via a website, **www.reallifeuniversity.com**, which contains a comment page for customer feedback.

CHANGE. I have seen change be both the success and the death knell of new business owners. Why? Some business owners think they need to change their products and approach constantly when all they really need to do is stick with the same decent product and excellent approach. Others need to change but are stuck in a rut or are afraid of risk. One of the best ways to see if your company needs to grow or change its approach is through the second "C"—customer service. Customers are always willing to tell you exactly what they want or don't want.

CHARITY. Never ever forget where you came from. Always be willing to donate part of your proceeds to some worthy charity. Why? Not only is it humanitarian and ethical, but also you show others that you are an honest business entrepreneur. The Giving Back Foundation has created a lot of good in the community, but it has also let people know who I am as a person and that I am a man who stands behind his word.

CHARACTER. Having personal integrity is the most important aspect of being a successful entrepreneur and often goes hand in hand with charity. Be ethical: Never cut corners, don't manipulate customers, and always do what you say you are going to do. In this day and age of Enron scandals and immoral CEOs, it is imperative that you show the business world that the next generation of entrepreneurs is going to run businesses the right way.

Once you have the five "C"s to success nailed down, you are ready to start running a successful and rewarding business. If you are anything like I was when I started my business, you are constantly dreaming up new ideas that you are positive will be successful business ventures—if only you can turn those dreams into realities! I would imagine that most business owners would agree with me in saying that their business started as a dream. It's time that you take advantage of that dream and turn it into a reality. In order to do that, just follow five simple steps that I have prepared for you:

D: Develop a plan
R: Recognize your potential
E: Explore your options
A: Activate your plan
M: Maintain a positive attitude

Develop a Plan

So you think you have this magnificent idea that will undoubtedly make you lots of money? Are you are confident that you have what it takes to be your own boss and manage a successful venture? Do you have a million questions about start-up funds, investors, supplies, target markets, pricing, and long-term goals? If you answered yes to any of the above questions, then it's time to turn your *idea* into a *reality*! A well-thought-out and developed business plan can help make this happen. The first and perhaps the most crucial step in starting your own business is developing a plan. Much like teachers use a lesson plan in their daily curriculum and architects use drawing plans to build structures, you must identify and develop your own plan for success—in business, it's called a business plan.

When I first came up with the concept of McMyne & Associates, LLC, every mentor I had ever had consistently encouraged me to develop a business plan. While I valued most of their advice, I nevertheless dismissed the importance of a business plan because I thought it would take too long and delay the opening of my company. This was my first big mistake. Without that plan in hand, no bank, client, or investor would even engage in a conversation with me. Whenever I was asked to present my business plan, I always replied, "I don't have it on paper, but it is in my head." Many times, that comment turned me into the laughingstock of the conversation.

While you may know exactly what you want to do and how you will go about doing it, this knowledge will not help you until you formulate it into a business plan on paper. No matter how big or how small your business is, you must have a plan. Your business plan not only will help you get in with potential investors and clients, but it also will provide you with structure and guidance.

When I finally sat down to begin writing my plan, I was intimidated by all the information I thought had to be included in my plan. While information such as a business strategy, market segmentation, market analysis, competition analysis, capital investments, capital equipment, and income projections may eventually be crucial for your plan, they are not necessary immediately. There are two critical sections that you should include in your initial plan:

1. A description of your business

2. Financial projections

If you start with those two basic sections, your plan will begin to serve its purpose: to guide you toward turning your *dream* into a *reality*. (If you'd like to see some good sample business plans, please check out this excellent government website for small business starters: **sba.gov/starting_business/ planning/writingplan.html**)

Recognize Your Potential

Perhaps the biggest mistake we make when we dream up a concept is self-doubt that we can actually achieve success. In order to be successful in business, you must first believe in yourself before you can expect others to believe in you. Sometimes we get a bit pessimistic and begin to see problems with our ideas; however, potential problems often turn into huge benefits. Let me give you an example.

When I was a freshman in college, I had this dream to write a book that would help future university students reach their fullest potential. Just about everyone that I associated with knew that I loved to write, but many of them discounted my idea of writing my own book because I am a severe dyslexic, and I am medicated for Attention Deficit Hyperactive Disorder. Many people in my life tried numerous times to talk me out of the book, telling me that I would never get it published. I wrote the first draft of the manuscript and eventually, after months of persuasion, got my former professor to join the team.

The value of having a professor as a co-author was astronomical. When referring back to my business plan, I realized that my goal was to help as many students avoid problems in their university experience. While writing the book alone could have very well accomplished that goal, I was confident that having a university professor as a co-author would offer a unique value to the book. We eventually wrote and published the first book geared to college students written by a current student and professor.

Despite the constant criticism and cynicism from those around me, I did not let it bring me down. I always recognized my ability to write and I knew—learning disabilities or no learning disabilities—I would succeed as an author if I really wanted to. You have to do the same—never give up on your dream. It is so important to recognize your ability in order to turn the dream into a reality early on in the process. If you are confident from the get-go that you can succeed, then do not let anything hold you back. Go at it head strong and use the potential problems as big opportunities, and never let pessimism get in your way!

Explore Your Options

It is very important that you always keep your eye on every door that has opened for you. It's easy to get caught up in quick and hasty decision-making, especially when you are just starting your business. Be very careful and do not let emotions get in your way. I found exploring all of my options logically to be a great benefit as a beginning entrepreneur.

When I started speaking, I was so excited about the opportunity to get agent representation that I did not allow myself adequate time to evaluate my options and choose the best agent to represent me. Rather, the first company that came knocking on my door was the company I chose; I immediately accepted their offer without exploring other options. Because of this hasty decision, I had to suffer for the duration of my one-year contract. The agency took advantage of me as a young entrepreneur, and ultimately the agency forced me to take two steps back in my career.

I bet that if you ask those around you who have had success in business, they can give you similar anecdotes to prove this point. Be careful with whom you deal with and *always* explore your options.

Activate Your Plan

After you have completely read this book written by some of the world's most-recognized student entrepreneurs, you will have the tools necessary to develop your dream into a reality by developing your plan for financial and personal success. Nevertheless, activating the plan is sometimes harder than developing it. Oftentimes, we come up with great ideas, but we are scared to make them happen. No matter what your fear may be, don't let it stand in your way. If you have taken the time and made the effort to develop a plan, now is the time to activate it.

A colleague of mine, Francis Bologna, best summed up fear in business when he told me, "Fear is nothing more than courage with a prayer." Don't let your fears stand in your way but instead let them be tools to help you in activating your plan.

Maintain a Positive Attitude

This final component of making your dream a reality is the most important as it encompasses who you should be as a person and how you should run your business. The only way you will be successful in turning your entrepreneurial dream into a reality is if you maintain the I CAN attitude rather than the I CAN'T attitude. Remember, the attitude that you portray on the outside will be the same attitude that those around you will respond to, and no one wants to work with someone who is an ogre. Sometimes, it will be hard to stay positive when the cards are not dealt the way you expect them to be, but don't let this get you down. Let your problems become your opportunities. After all, in entrepreneurship, the glass must always be full!

The Key is Happiness

Courtney Hennessey
Codi Jewelry

Mid-Mississippi Region
Regional Partner:
Saint Louis University

Courtney Hennessey

Courtney Diane Hennessey is a 24-year-old designer from St. Louis, Missouri. Codi is the name of her line of jewelry, which was derived from the first two letters of her first and middle name. Hennessey unintentionally stumbled upon the career of jewelry design in December, 1999. At the same time, she was a 21-year-old full-time student at Saint Louis University. She had just gotten out of school for a month at Christmas break and decided to keep busy by making fun jewelry. Being the creative type, Hennessey strung some bracelets and necklaces and sparkled around town in her creations. In no time, she had passed out five hundred business cards, and people began calling her house asking for the "jewelry girl."

Since then, her business has taken off, and her jewelry is adorned and adored by such stylish women as Brooke Shields and Kelly Ripa. Codi Jewelry was featured on the popular morning talk show "LIVE with Regis and Kelly" and can be found in the cases of upscale boutiques in Aspen, Palm Beach, and New York City. Hennessey won the North American Collegiate Entrepreneur Award in 2001 as a result of her successful business. Says Hennessey, "I have found my passion. I feel that in life if you can discover your niche—something that you truly enjoy doing—success will inevitably follow, and you have found one of the keys to happiness."

Codi Jewelry

FOUNDER: Courtney Hennessey
WEB: codijewelry.com
EMAIL: courtney@codijewelry.com
PHONE: 877/808-9888
ADDRESS: 1423 Andrew Dr.
Warson Woods MO 63122

S chool's out!

It was December 9, 1999. I had just finished my last midterm, and I had no idea that this particular day was going to document the first day of my unintended career in jewelry design. I was twenty-two years old and in my third year of undergraduate school at Saint Louis University. We were out for a month on Christmas break, which to me meant lots of free time to spend doing what I like to do. (This is key #1: As a young entrepreneur, you will succeed if you pursue a business doing what you like to do.) With that sense of freedom guiding the way, I headed straight to the bead shop. This was when those stretchy crystal bracelets were "in": remember when people would wear several of them at a time in all different colors? Well, instead of buying each bracelet for ten bucks a pop, I thought I'd make some myself. That was my intention at least.

I decided to go to a neighborhood bead store and was instantly bombarded with myriads of beads and crystals of every shape, size, and color. I went crazy; I felt like a kid in a candy store. My initial idea of buying a few crystals for a stretchy bracelet turned into a four hundred dollar investment—on my dad's credit card! (Key #2: Having a venture capitalist who is also a family member really helps!) I walked out with an upset feeling in my stomach as I had never spent that kind of money before in one place, especially without asking Dad. My plan was to save the receipt and pay Dad back as soon as I made enough money selling the stretchy bracelets I intended to make. The timing could not have been more perfect considering that it was the ninth of December, peak holiday shopping season. So, I strung a few bracelets together with the crystals and new findings I had just discovered. I wore my fun, new creations around town and the orders immediately began pouring in. I knew I had something when I brought my "T-bar" of samples (about twenty different styles) to my great aunt's wake (my mom's brilliant suggestion—to get the family's mind off the matter) and left with eight hundred dollars in orders. (Key #3: Opportunity may strike when you least expect it—even at funerals!) At fifteen dollars a bracelet, there were a lot of bracelets to string before Christmas. And that was just the beginning of it; orders continued to pour in through the holidays. Word of mouth spread the news about Codi all over St. Louis. It was a great place to start something as it is a "small big town" where people are close-knit and talk about anything new to the area. All new customers served as walking advertisements whenever they wore my creations. Whether at the register at the grocery store or mingling at a cocktail party, everyone it seemed would comment on the jewelry. "I love your necklace; where did you find that?" "Oh, I made it, have a card!" And the dominos continued to fall.

It got to me a little bit when I'd be up until 3:00 A.M. on Friday and Saturday stringing jewelry while all my high school friends, who were in from out of town, were at the bars. (Key #4: Take full advantage of good timing—and bad timing.) But, I realized that duty was calling, and people were enjoying the products I was creating. Therefore, I kept on stringing.

As with the start of every business, obstacles inevitably pop up that need to be overcome. A few weeks after Christmas, a couple of phone calls came in from upset customers whose bracelets had snapped. I anxiously reassured them I would fix them right away. After several more calls came in concerning broken bracelets, I knew something needed to be done to fix this reccurring problem. (Key #5: No business is successful with a product that breaks.) I was getting sick of restringing bracelets I had already strung once. I had no time for that!

I fixed the problem by taking the quality of my jewelry to the next level. I invested in a sturdy, flexible wire made for jewelry making, three tools, and a lot of crimps. (To all you jewelry novices, crimps are the essential component needed to finish off any piece of jewelry.) This definitely solved my first problem. It also allowed me to use more expensive stones and components in my design. I got into all sorts of semi-precious stones, freshwater pearls, Bali silver, sterling silver, and Swarovski crystals. I also tagged everything with a sterling heart as my signature. (Key #5: Have a trademark or at least something that sets your product off from the rest.) This quickly raised the quality and price-point of my jewelry a great deal. It was no longer costume jewelry; now it was designer or fashion jewelry. Next, it was time to come up with a name for this emerging line of jewelry I was creating. After many suggestions and racking my brain, I finally decided on Codi Jewelry. It was cute, catchy, sophisticated, and easy to remember. It was also special since it was personal: The name Codi comes from the first two letters of my first and middle name, Courtney Diane. Diane is also my mom's name; she's by far my greatest saleswoman, not to mention walking advertisement. (Key #6: It's nice when names of companies have a story or meaning behind them.) At this time, I also thought of a slogan that would grab people's attention. It would be "Funky for day, fancy for night." This explains how the same piece of jewelry could be worn casually during the day and dressed up at night. So Codi was born, and the business cards were printed and gone shortly thereafter.

A few months after the holidays, I got a call from a Neiman Marcus associate. She had finally tracked down my card after seeing whatever this "Codi Jewelry" was on several of her customers. She suggested that I show my designs to the designer jewelry manager. That I did, and a Neiman Marcus Codi trunk show was immediately booked for that September. I was thrilled and continued to work on my designs through the summer in preparation for the debut. Nothing else in the entire department sold that day except Codi Jewelry. People were three deep surrounding the counter. With that, a second show was booked a couple months later for November holiday shopping. Between the two shows, I sold twenty thousand dollars' worth of Codi Jewelry.

By this time, I had rearranged my schedule of classes (I was taking seventeen hours as all of this was unfolding) so that I could go to school in the mornings and do business in the afternoons. I would take home appointments at my parents' house, where I had transformed their dining room into a store. Word spread quickly locally and after the successful trunk shows, Neiman Marcus decided to carry Codi Jewelry in their cases. Doing the trunk shows at Neiman Marcus was great exposure and brand/product association. (Key #7: If you have the chance to associate your company with a well-known established one, take it!)

I was finishing up my last year at SLU when one of my classmates told me about the North American Collegiate Entrepreneur Award. I applied and ended up winning first place for my region, which includes Missouri, Kentucky, and Tennessee. I advanced to the finals and won the award for "Creativity and Innovation." Obtaining this caliber of a continental award resulted in tons of local press and recognition, including news shows, radio interviews, and numerous articles. (Key #8: Take advantage of free press and publicity; it's extremely pricey to pay for that kind of exposure.)

Shortly thereafter, I graduated from SLU in 2001 with a degree in communications. After graduating, I decided to move to Aspen, Colorado, where I met my future husband, Mike Hopson. Business continued to flourish, and I only became busier and busier. Mike had graduated from the University of Colorado in 1999 with a degree in finance, and he was the perfect candidate to take over that side of the business. (Key #10: Marry your future CFO. Key #11: If you can work with 'em, you can do just about anything with 'em!) This enabled my production to double since I had much more time to spend in the design and stringing. He ran the left-brained side of the business and I concentrated completely on the right. Since Mike had spent the former four years as a caddy in Aspen, he introduced me to all of the people he knew there. One customer led to others, and Aspen proved to be quite the market. From there we moved to Jupiter, Florida, where many of the summer "Aspenites" were from. We continued to set up home parties with our Aspen connections and were able to sell Codi Jewelry to several local boutiques along the coast from Palm Beach to Boca Raton. We spent seven months in Florida, which has been our best market yet. We think it's because there is a high level of disposable income there, people seem to always be in vacation mode, and the jewelry looks the best on a nice tan!

Something else very exciting took place during our time spent down South. I decided to take Mike to the Bahamas for his birthday, February 20. I strategically planned this as I knew that the morning talk show "LIVE with Regis and Kelly" was going to be broadcasting live from the Bahamas that same week. I am a big fan of the show, and I watch it constantly every morning when I am making jewelry. I always thought Kelly was so cute and would be a perfect model for Codi Jewelry. I was determined to somehow get it on her. Coincidently, the first place we went after landing in the sunny Bahamas was to have lunch, and it happened to be where Regis was staying. He also happened to have just gotten off the tennis courts and was about to enjoy some lunch himself with his wife and daughters, and I happened to have my jewelry with me since I did not want to leave it with the bellman at the hotel! I decided to have a Bloody Mary, which definitely gave me the courage to go up to his table and introduce myself. (Key #12: A little alcohol never hurts!) I pretty much laid my jewelry out on their table and told them who I was. After they got over the interference, they actually took a great interest in my story and my little business I had going. They were very nice and asked me lots of questions to learn more about my background. I ended up talking to them for about twenty minutes and gave them bracelets as a souvenir because they were so nice. I also gave Regis a necklace to give to Kelly.

The next morning, Mike and I went to the show. We were in the audience before the show was about to start when I spotted the box containing the necklace I had given him on their table where they sit to do the show. My heart dropped, and my stomach tied in knots. I didn't even want to tell Mike what I saw so I wouldn't jinx anything in case it was not the box I thought it was. Sure enough, they came out, sat down, and within the first few minutes of talking back and forth, Regis decided to tell the story of my coming up to his table and giving him this necklace to give to Kelly. He even spelled out Codi, C-O-D-I, which was huge, since most people would assume it would be Cody with a "Y." He gave her the necklace. She immediately put it on, thanked me, and then wore it the entire show. That following week, I got 103,000 hits on my website. Talk about nice free advertising! It was definitely one of the cooler things that had ever happened to me. Good thing I had no fear and introduced myself, or should I say, thank goodness for that Bloody Mary!

From there, we decided to check out the other coast and took the business to Los Angeles. We only lasted the summer in L.A. because the traffic was horrible, everything was too spread out, and it was lacking that good ol' nice Midwestern attitude. (Key #13: Surround yourself with good people.) So, with that in mind, we moved back home to St. Louis and got engaged. We thought it made sense to come back home, first of all because my whole family lives there, second, because it is where I started the business and it had made somewhat of a name for itself, and third, because it was centrally located and conducive to travel. After a year and a half of promoting Codi Jewelry in the east, west, and in between, we had accumulated customers all over the United States, and a centrally located base sounded like a good idea.

During our travels, we had also sold Codi Jewelry to fifteen upscale boutiques nationwide, which was all I could handle supplying on top of the everyday orders. We developed our website **www.codijewelry.com** and filled orders from that as well. *Palm Beach Illustrated,* a well-known upscale magazine, did a full-page cameo on Codi Jewelry and me, which also reached a wide array of potential customers and was wonderful publicity. Word was spreading fast, and I continued to string.

Business doubled the year Mike joined the Codi team and it has doubled each year since. Currently, we are maxed out between the two of us working with the business. I think the time has finally come that I'm going to need some help stringing.

Settled back home, we spend a great deal of our time traveling doing home trunk shows since we have customers everywhere whose friends are now wanting to see the jewelry. I also continue to take orders off the website, and when I am at home, I take home appointments. Presently, I am working on branding my product. I custom-designed a heart that is being manufactured in sterling silver and stamped with my Codi logo. I am going to trademark this tag so that if anyone copies my designs, people will know it is only a "real" Codi piece if it has the Codi trademarked heart. Once my pieces are tagged, I'm going to send them to an upscale department store in hopes that they supply their nationwide locations with Codi Jewelry. I will continue to get it in as many high-end boutiques as possible. If and when this happens, I will become the designer/overseer, and my employees will be in charge of the mass production. I will still design and make the one-of-a-kind pieces and the new styles for each season, but I won't have to spend any more time filling orders. This way, I'll have more time to focus on designing new pieces, which is what I enjoy most.

With that in mind, I'd have to say that the key to success is finding something you enjoy doing. Start by figuring out what that is for you. I have found through my hobby-turned-business that if you're doing something you like, it doesn't feel like work. And who wants to work their whole life? Doing something you love to do will also make you happy. If you are happy, you are successful.

Acknowledgment

I feel it is only appropriate at this time to thank my fiancé, Mike. Without him, I can honestly say that Codi Jewelry would not be what it is today. His support and motivation have taken this business to the next level and allowed me to enjoy every step of the way. He is an integral part of our success, and I can't wait to spend the rest of my life with him and see what happens next!

Working Big

Roberto Arzola-Mejías
RCAM Computers

Caribbean Region
Regional Partner: International
Entrepreneurship Institute

Roberto Arzola-Mejías

Roberto Carlos Arzola-Mejías was born in 1977 in Ponce, Puerto Rico. He grew up in the barrio of Macaná del Río in the nearby town of Guayanilla, and upon his graduation from high school, he received the leadership and citizenship medal from the mayor and was recognized as the school's most outstanding electronics student. He enrolled in the University of Puerto Rico, Ponce branch, in 1995, quickly becoming captain of a basketball team, a volunteer with disabled children, and a member of the college chorus. His music talents won him the prize for voice in Puerto Rico's Fama Festival in 1996, and singing engagements provided him with a source of income. He left school when his second part-time job in a computer company became a full-time endeavor. When the company closed in 1998, he immediately launched his own computer sales and repair business.

By 2000, RCAM Computers was earning enough to rent offices and hire two full-time and two part-time employees. Although he continued to manage the company, he also returned to the university to pursue a degree in elementary education. A member of both the youth band's trombone section and the church choir, he continued his work with disabled children and was recognized as the town's "Outstanding Young Person" by the Guayanilla Lions Club. Roberto Arzola received his degree in education from the University of Puerto Rico in June 2003.

RCAM Computers

FOUNDER:	Roberto Arzola-Mejías
WEB:	rcamcomputers.com
EMAIL:	rcamcomp@coqui.net
PHONE:	787/812-4221
ADDRESS:	Urb. Star Light Calle Novas 3018 Ponce PR 00717

E ver since I was a kid, being told I couldn't do something has had the opposite effect. I think, "I'll show them!" Then I do. There are always opportunities around.

I was born in one of the poorest neighborhoods in the south coast town of Ponce, Puerto Rico. By the time I was three or four, I was driving my mother crazy. I was always on the move, and a doctor told me I wouldn't be able to go to kindergarten with my twin brother because I couldn't sit still long enough to learn anything. Fortunately, my mother sought a second opinion, and that doctor told her I was normal, just hyperactive. Nevertheless, I learned to read by the time I was five. I loved electrical things, and I read a book on electricity written by one of my relatives and started fixing toys and radios and Christmas lights for people in my neighborhood, Macaná del Río, Guayanilla. But my first real business—collecting and selling aluminum cans to help my family with a little extra income—started when I was twelve.

Then, when I was in the ninth grade, my brother broke the finger off a statue at school. I was blamed for the damage, and by the time it was sorted out, the teacher who owned the piece told us both that we were good-for-nothings who would never amount to anything and probably end up in jail. It was a defining moment for me because right then I decided I would do something to show her she was wrong and that I could make something of my life. I graduated from high school with a vocational degree in electronics. I was at the top of my class and received a medal from the mayor for citizenship and leadership.

It was the same in college; I enrolled in the University of Puerto Rico at the Ponce campus. The first time I had to get up and speak in front of a class, it was a disaster. I was nervous, and the professor ripped into me. He told me that I didn't belong there and that he was ashamed to have a kid like me in his class. Instead of giving up, I redoubled my efforts. I graduated magna cum laude, and already I have a successful business that has been running for five years.

Starting a Company

When I started college, I had sent my resumé to a company to get a part-time job in equipment maintenance, but the owner wanted to hire me as a technician instead. He knew I didn't know computers, but he said he wouldn't pay me for a month so that I could take the time to learn. This is what I mean by opportunity. I worked in my free time between classes and Saturdays and holidays. He not only started paying me after that first month, but before too long, he made me chief technician with a good salary.

It was a good job, so I left college to work full time. I learned the business, but the company ran into trouble and closed down just before Christmas in 1998. I was paying $375 on my car loan every month, and I had only $200 in the bank. I needed to do something quickly. Since I knew computers by then, I opened my own business for repairing them three days after my employer closed down. This is how RCAM (for Roberto Carlos Arzola-Mejías) Computers began.

I didn't have a computer of my own, so I went to a friend's house on a Saturday to make flyers for RCAM Computers. We spread them around the parking lots at a couple of shopping centers. I put a beeper number on the flyer since I didn't have a phone. It was tough with no phone and working out of my bedroom, but a few people knew me from my previous job, and friends from school brought me their computers to fix. After that, it was word of mouth that helped the business to get known. By the end of the month, I had enough money to make my car payment. I also had a contract for singing at a nearby hotel as a backup job.

After a while, I heard that the local Department of Education was going out to bid on a contract to supply computers, so I decided to go for it. A friend told me, "You're a nobody; you can't win a contract like that!" So I decided that if I were nobody, then it was important to look like somebody. I got five of my friends to dress in suits and carry briefcases and go with me to the auction. I didn't have any money to buy computers, but I knew what they should cost. And ever since I bombed my first speech in that negative professor's class, I always prepare quotes and presentations very carefully. When the people saw six of us, they didn't know our briefcases were empty, along with our pockets. They said, "Who is that guy? RCAM Computers must be a really big company if they can let five extra people leave work to come to an auction!"

I won the bid, and then I had to figure out how to buy the computers. When my bank turned me down for a loan, the bank officer told me to give up; nobody would give me, a 21-year-old kid, a business loan. So I went to another bank. It was Secretaries Day, and the loan officer told me she had to take her secretaries out, so I should come back Monday. As it happens, she took them to the hotel where I had a job singing. That was luck, but it created a positive impression of me as a hard-working person. I figured I'd never have such a good opportunity again. This officer didn't want to give me the loan, either, but I used psychology on her. I told her what the other bank said, and I challenged her to prove them wrong. In the end, she went to the assistant manager and together they agreed to lend me eight thousand dollars and to establish my account, which allowed me to buy the computers. Those bank officers and that loan were what really established my business.

People ask me how I dared to go after that contract. But who could compete with my price? I didn't have any overhead—no office, no employees, just me. My motto is "Be

Small, But Work Big." You have to take risks to get ahead. I started out watching the big companies' advertising offers so that I could better them. The bid for this contract was the same, just on a bigger scale.

Growing the Business

After that first contract, I began buying computers for individual people, but then I discovered that many of my potential customers just couldn't afford them. So I went to the savings and loan cooperative in my neighborhood to see if they would finance them for their customers. That worked out really well because they let me put a few computer setups there so that when somebody came in to deposit their money, they would see them, want one, and get financing on the spot to buy my computers. The cooperative was my showroom, and it didn't cost me anything!

But I really needed another, steadier source of customers. I already learned that people who can get the financing are the ones who buy computers, so I started visiting the local branch of AEELA (Association of Puerto Rico Government Employees), which is the agency that makes loans to government workers. I kept visiting the local office but was getting nowhere, so I jumped in my car and drove to the main office in San Juan, Puerto Rico's capital. I didn't have an appointment, but I convinced the receptionist to let me see the person in charge. She felt sorry for me because I had driven all that way.

AEELA's granting me a contract was a big achievement. The government is the biggest employer in Puerto Rico. RCAM became one of its only five authorized computer suppliers, which meant that anybody in the south coast who was working for the central or a municipal government who wanted to buy a computer on installment had to come to me, and I was ready and waiting!

As for the repair and technical side of the business, for two years I worked by myself out of my bedroom. After regular working hours, I went to people's homes to fix computers, and I usually worked until ten or eleven at night. I always gave the repair customers the first job free. I'd say, "If you're happy with the work, then recommend me." I believe if you want to start earning, first you have to give something and prove yourself. Then people come back, and they bring their friends.

My mother kept telling me I was killing myself, but between the sales and the setup and repair, in two years I had enough business that I could afford to rent office space and hire a secretary and a technician. Brenda Santos and José Romero started with me then and are still with the company. They freed up some of my time, which gave me another opportunity. I still believed in having some sort of professional preparation. I had done volunteer work teaching computers to kids, and I liked that a lot. Now I could go back to school, this time to major in elementary education at the university.

I've won prizes for academic achievement, and because of my business, I received the award from the International Entrepreneurship Institute in Puerto Rico. Winning and traveling to the United States to compete nationally has given me a lot of publicity in Puerto Rico. It showed people that my business was real and growing and that I wasn't just a student playing around with computers! Before I graduated, I made enough money in the business to be able to buy the building where I had been renting, which was a credibility milestone.

So I have shown that I can be a successful student and a run a business at the same time, and now that I have graduated, people keep asking me what I'm going to do next. I don't know for sure. Although my company already makes a profit, there are a lot of opportunities to expand the business. On the other hand, in my heart, I'm a teacher. Perhaps I'll do both: Run my business and be a teacher, which is what I already did by managing the business while I was a student. Maybe that will help to keep the hyperactive kid in me busy!

Just Do Something!

Andy and Chad Baker
CashCard Coupon Company

Ohio Valley Region
Regional Partner:
John Carroll University

Andy and Chad Baker

The Baker Twins work twice as hard! That's their advertising slogan, but if these young entrepreneurs had a signature bumper sticker, it might read, "Born to Hustle."

Chad and Andy Baker went into business for themselves in grade school, selling pencils. Later, they took advantage of a student strike at the cafeteria at their Nashville, Tennessee, high school. The twins piled all their books into one locker and stocked the other with food, which they sold to customers who chose not to patronize the school food line.

The Bakers started their first college business in Bloomington, Indiana, a week before they registered at Indiana University. They sold advertising to businesses and distributed their Cash Cards free to students. The Cash Card is a small coupon card that conveniently fits in wallets or purses. The card is free to students, but advertisers must pay to be on the card. Cardholders use the card an unlimited number of times, thus building customer loyalty at participating stores. The twins also have a gumball machine business with machines in Nashville and Indiana.

The twins currently operate a manufacturing and distribution business. They manufacture distinctive signs predominantly for restaurants and bars. The signs are used to advertise daily specials or other important information to customers. The items Chad and Andy Baker distribute are also geared toward the restaurant and bar industry. So far, the twins have sold their products in almost every state, and they have customers in Ireland, Puerto Rico, Hawaii, and Russia.

CashCard Coupon Company

FOUNDERS: The Baker Twins
WEB: bakertwins.com
PHONE: 812/337-TWIN
ADDRESS: P.O. Box 2176
Bloomington IN 47402

A s early as we can remember, Andy and I have been hard working and entrepreneurial. At a very young age, our divorced and feuding parents provided a great source of inspiration and motivation for us. Whenever we needed money, the parent we approached would point the finger at the other parent. Our mother would say, "Your father is the one with all of the money; go ask him." Our father would say "I give your mother child support; go ask her." They provided us with most of what we wanted, but we soon realized that making money on our own made the best sense. This desire to make it on our own has continued throughout our lives. Andy and I decided early on that even if we made less owning our own business, we never wanted to have to settle for a nine-to-five job. We wanted to be responsible for our own destiny. Working for ourselves, we could never blame a boss for holding us back.

As young children, we did most of the usual young entrepreneurial businesses: lemonade stands, car washing, dog walking, etc. One of our first ventures that actually had great potential was the vending business. We teamed up with a very close friend and purchased a few candy machines. We placed the machines anywhere we could. We started off by approaching family friends with restaurants, dry cleaners, car washes, and other high-traffic areas. We then approached the owners of stores that we regularly frequented and asked that they let us place a machine in their business. Typically we had to give a percentage of the profits to store owner, but some of our family friends let us keep one hundred percent! The machines turned out to be a great business; we still own vending machines eight years after setting up our first route. When we first entered into the vending business, we called friends of our father who had set up a huge vending route in Atlanta. Our father's friends told us the most profitable types of candy to vend, the best machines, the worst machines, and even provided us with contacts at vending companies. Using their knowledge, we were able to avoid purchasing low-quality machines. Many of the original machines we purchased so long ago are still out on location today.

The machines were perfect for us; they required very little capital to purchase, and they didn't require much time. We could fill the machine with candy and let it sit for almost six weeks before we had to check it. We made sure to clean the machines very well each time we checked them, but the entire process took up very little time. This business was also very easy to grow and didn't take much capital to do so. Most of the machines were small, three-section machines that held Mike & Ikes, M&Ms, gum, or a similar candy. The machines took only quarters and in return would give customers a handful of candy. In addition, they were small and light enough that we could fit them in any car. Until obtaining a Small Business Administration loan, we had always focused on starting businesses that required very little cash but a lot of sweat equity. This is an excellent way to get started. If you don't invest lots of money, it's impossible to lose lots of money. Raising money even when times are good is very difficult. If you can start a business with few resources—even if that business is not going to grow into a major company—it is an excellent stepping-stone just to have gained experience from starting something.

We moved on to other ventures from a DJ business to a grocery delivery business for the elderly. Nothing was taking off, but people started to notice how ambitious we were. People did notice our ambition, but we made sure to remind them. Networking is one of the most important things any entrepreneur can do. Every time we were in the press, we sent a copy of the article to hundreds of people. We wanted to be fresh on people's minds, and we wanted them to know how hard we were working. Even now as we travel from trade show to trade show, we make it a point to send postcards to our bankers, mentors, and friends. In addition, we learned from each and every idea we tried out.

One thing that we learned from the vending business was how hard having a business partner can be. Our relationship with our vending partner greatly deteriorated while we were in business together. It seems that partnerships usually end up with one person feeling he or she works more than the other. Unless you're lucky enough to have an identical twin with your exact same work ethic, we suggest you do your venture on your own. Definitely seek out the expertise of individuals in the field and consult your mentors; however, don't take on a partner unless you absolutely have to. We learned an important lesson when we nearly lost a friend because of what we thought would be a fun venture together.

Making sure people noticed our hard work paid off when we were raising money for our manufacturing business. When we approached a wealthy family friend to invest, he was more than willing to do so for fifty-one percent of the company. We felt giving up total control was out of the question, so we started shopping for a bank loan. Fortunately, most of the bankers we met with were familiar with the Baker Twins or some of our products. Our reputation preceded us and gave us credibility with a lending institution, even though we were young. One key thing a bank likes is a history of sales. Unfortunately, our products were new and had no proven track record, thus making our sales job even more important. It turned out we did a good enough sales job to get the loan. Our first loan was from a small local bank in Indiana. We were shocked and thrilled when we received fifty thousand dollars for our manufacturing and distribution business.

Once Andy and I started college, we decided to revitalize a business with which a friend had been successful while in college almost ten years earlier. Our friend provided us with his old promotional materials and gave us insight on how to operate the business. The Cash Card was a basically like the coupon cards that high schools sell for fundraisers. Our approach and distribution was much different from most cards, thus giving us an advantage over our competitors. Most high schools sell coupon cards; they may distribute a few thousand cards. Our card was free and we guaranteed advertisers forty thousand cards. The high school cards were free to advertise on, but the distribution was nothing to speak of. We charged hundreds of dollars to be on our card, but the intense distribution made it worthwhile to our customers.

The business took off with a lot of hard work, and then we decided to expand into the bathroom. Just like our friend who taught us about the Cash Card, we sought out someone to teach us about restroom advertising. We actually found an individual via the Internet. While researching the business, we came across an article about an individual who had started a restroom advertising business with his brother. We quickly contact the brothers in Florida and told them our goals and objectives. We were very excited when they agreed to discuss the business via conference calls. Had it not been for the brothers in Florida, we would have made many costly mistakes, such as buying the wrong types of advertising frames. Bathroom or restroom advertising was a concept that was very well known in our hometown of Nashville, but it was new to our college town of Bloomington, Indiana. The restroom adverting paid a few bills, but it never took off like we thought it would. Although we never made the kind of money we expected with Your-N-Sight, we did successfully barter for all sorts of great items.

We have found in every business that we have been involved with that people don't like to let go of their money. If you can figure out a way to trade services, you may still end up with something of great value, even if it's not in the form of cash. We exchanged advertising for a 36" flat-screen TV, car washes, meals at numerous restaurants, printing, and even flooring tile. We would have never dropped the kind of money a 36" flat-screen TV cost, but given the opportunity to barter, we jumped on it.

After dropping out of college at the beginning of our senior year, we began manufacturing a very unique sign that is now being used by restaurants all over the world. The sign has two main components: a light source and a piece of acrylic. The acrylic slides directly under the light source, which illuminates the acrylic. Restaurateurs use a special paint marker to write on the acrylic. The writing then glows, drawing attention from customers. The magic of the sign is that the light source is so small that people can't figure out where the light is coming from. In addition, we began importing unique items from France, Canada, and Spain. We sold the product at trade shows all over the country.

People always tell us that they think it's great how we work for ourselves and create out our own destiny. People also always tell us how they have great ideas, but it's just not the right time, they don't have the money, or they don't have the time. The problem with most budding entrepreneurs is that they are not willing to take the risks necessary to be successful. They don't get outside of their box and go for it. One statement that some of our mentors said that struck us was this: It's not necessarily the idea that makes the business successful; it's the people. This statement could not be truer. As you have read, we have had numerous businesses; all of them have had some level of success. Had we not pressed on with what was once a mere idea, we would have never gotten anywhere.

We are extremely hard working, determined, and we are going to make ourselves successful. Granted, there is a certain amount of luck that is involved, but do you think Bill Gates would not be successful in another venture? In fact, we personally believe that luck is when preparation and opportunity meet. The trick is to go out, do something, and throw yourself into it. Remember, the harder you work, the luckier you get! One problem that we have had is jumping around from idea to idea. We mainly did that because we had to do what paid the bills, but now we are in a position where we can focus on the manufacturing and distribution industry. This industry is broad enough where we can have several products and be very diverse while still maintaining our focus.

Although each business venture we have encountered has been somewhat different, all have given us contacts that we can use in the future. For example, when we were in the restroom advertising business, we commissioned an acrylic and plastics company to build acrylic frames to hold our advertisements. Three years later, when we started Indoor Signs, we already had a list of acrylic distributors. One of the people we had approached years earlier about the restroom frames had been very rude to us. We had made a note of our experience with the company, and ironically enough, they approached us about selling us acrylic for our sign business. We pulled out our notes about their past service when we were informed that the employee who had been so rude to us was still with the company. We made sure to inform the sales rep that we were not interested in working with a company that had been so disrespectful years earlier. This story should serve as a reminder that people do remember how you treat them.

On the flip side, just as poor service is remembered, so is great service. At one of our first trade shows, we sold some of our products to a man named Rodney Wasserstrom in

Columbus, Ohio. We had just started our business, and our delivery times were very slow. Mr. Wasserstrom had not received the signs he ordered months earlier, so we decided to offer him free passes to an upcoming trade show in his area. We felt bad that our service was so poor, and we wanted him to gain access to the show for free. We sent Mr. Wasserstrom a letter explaining this, and we told him we hoped to see him at the show. As we drove in to Columbus, Ohio, for our show, we passed a huge building that said Wasserstrom Super Store on the side. At that point, we started to wonder if this was the same Wasserstrom we knew. Once we made it to the convention center and unloaded, we saw a huge booth called Wasserstrom. It turned out this individual who we thought owned a small restaurant actually owned a business with sales just under two hundred fifty million dollars a year. Mr. Wasserstrom got a huge kick out of the letter and has since become a mentor and a great customer! As an entrepreneur, you never know what industry you will be in later on in life, so it is extremely important to not unnecessarily burn bridges.

The two most important ideas you can take from this chapter are learning from the best and doing something. We always seek our best people in a given field when we get involved in that field. If we can't find an advisor, we go to someone else with more general experience than us.

If you are not aware of anyone to advise you, just contact your local Chamber of Commerce or pick up a newspaper. We have found that simply sending a letter explaining that you are interested in some advice normally elicits an "I would be happy to meet with you" response. There are always going to be people out there who are smarter than you, so there is no point in recreating the wheel. The goal in business is not to work the hardest or the most hours. The goal is to be extremely profitable and efficient. We have found that turning to other people and learning from them is an extremely valuable way to learn.

Currently, our best mentors are two brothers who own a company that leases modular trailers to businesses that need more storage. We found them through an article in *Inc.* magazine. We did some research and found out they too had attended IU. We sent them a letter asking for a meeting, and they called back and met with us. Since then, we have met with them for advice on a fairly regular basis. We are very lucky to be able to pick up the phone and get advice from guys running a forty-two million-dollar business that started with less than fifty thousand dollars. Their field of expertise has very little to do with our industry, but they help provide us with feedback when we encounter obstacles. They have also surrounded themselves with successful people in other industries. They actually introduced us to a friend of theirs who is involved in manufacturing. This contact ultimately helped us design and purchase a product from China.

The theory of six degrees of separation is extremely true and valuable. If you surround yourself with other successful people, you will surely find people who can be excellent resources. It is vital to learn from others but also remember that there is no secret formula. To us, much of the fun in business is the fact that you can run things your own way.

Remember that even if you have thousands of great ideas, they will never make you a penny if they just stay on paper. Do whatever you have to do to get started. If you can't pick an idea, throw a dart at your list and run with the one it hits. It's not so much the idea as the person behind the idea. Milton Hershey failed many times before coming up with the chocolate company we all know and love. If your first idea is not a success, take the lessons you learned from your first business and go back to your list for the next idea.

You CAN DO It, Too!

William Barrett
Waterwood Wonders

Mid-Mississippi Region
Regional Partner:
Saint Louis University

William Barrett

Entrepreneurship started early for William Barrett. In the third grade, he sold cinnamon-coated toothpicks to classmates. Though little money was earned, it was clear entrepreneurship was in his blood.

William was born June 15, 1981, to James Barrett and Linda Francis. In 1999, after working at Bristol Motor Speedway, he noticed a need for specialized cleaning services that catered to sporting events. Later that year, he started Can Do Enterprises. With his Can Do spirit, he quickly secured contracts and successfully competed against more established companies. In 2000, William placed third regionally in the North American Collegiate Entrepreneur Contest. Can Do Enterprises was primarily a seasonal business, and to help diversify, he started Waterwood Wonders in 2000. Waterwood Wonders was based on his hobby of making furniture from driftwood. Waterwood Wonders takes driftwood harvested from the lakes of northeast Tennessee and converts this wood into functional works of art for a customer's home. In 2001, William placed first regionally for his business in the National American Collegiate Entrepreneur awards. William's latest venture is Barrett Investment Group, a real-estate development company that specializes in residential development. William is currently a finance major with a construction minor at East Tennessee State University. He has taken the lessons learned from college and applied them to his latest venture. William continues to think BIG with Barrett Investment Group and looks forward to a bright future.

Waterwood Wonders

FOUNDER: William Barrett
EMAIL: williambarrett@hotmail.com
PHONE: 423/791-3843
ADDRESS: 209 Allison Court
Piney Flats TN 37686

Why am I an entrepreneur? It would be easy to go to work for someone else and pull that nine-to-five drill, but it would be unrewarding. When you work for someone, they profit off your hard work, but when you work for yourself, you profit off your own talents and ambitions. I would much rather profit off myself. Nevertheless, owning a business can be a challenge. Though the potential for more money is exciting, it will not get you through the hard times. Motivation must come from something greater than money; motivation comes from the challenge of the business and the sense of accomplishment you get from growing a business.

In one of the businesses that I own, Can Do Enterprises, I have made more money than I would have working for another cleaning company. However, I have been involved in contracts that have lost money. For example, I once placed a bid on cleaning a facility after a local car race. It did not take long before I realized that I was losing money. I had underbid the job. It is sometimes hard to stay motivated and enthusiastic about the given job when you know in the back of your mind that you are losing money. Although I underbid, I tried to remember that when starting a business, never count how much money is being made per hour. Why? When you concentrate on how much money you are making, you may lessen your dedication to the venture if profits are initially low. Remember that by growing a business, you are creating something that has monetary value. Whether it is equipment or supplies or even a company's good will, they have a marketable value that can be sold later. Motivation cannot be extrinsically influenced; rather, it must come from some sort of intrinsic value. For example, I have a driftwood furniture business called Waterwood Wonders. It is extremely rewarding, though it is not as financially rewarding as my other projects. The joy I receive comes from making something beautiful out of a worn and weathered stump.

The part I enjoy most about being an entrepreneur is the challenge before me; money is just a measuring stick. The challenge of running a business allows me to test my abilities, and it gives me control of my future. Achievement is directly related to the effort I put in it. In Can Do Enterprises, sales increase when I make attempts to get more contracts. Effort will take you far; however, even some of the most ambitious people derail their own success because they look for it in the wrong places. When you work for a company, you are creating success for that company, but that is not necessarily creating success for you. Companies do not always have your best interest at heart, but you do have your best interest at heart. People go through life following a set course. They go to high school because they are supposed to. Then they continue to college because that is what they are told is the right thing to do. They want to be successful, but they expect it to come to them. They think working for a company is the answer. Owning a business gives me a chance to do more and be more. People wait for success to find them, and in return, success never reaches their feet. Make your own success and build your own entrepreneurial dream.

Who are the entrepreneurs? They are the dreamers, the curious, the daring. As children, they drive their parents crazy asking questions, taking things apart, and sometimes appearing to just ignore them all together, but in reality they are lost in their imagination, traveling on roads of the mind that others seldom even know exist. A wise teacher or parent will not scold these children but instead encourage them, for these children are the entrepreneurs of the future. Einstein once said, "Imagination is more important than knowledge." Entrepreneurs think outside the box, and their imagination allows them to see things in a different way.

In the third grade I started my first business. I sold cinnamon-coated toothpicks to my classmates. I did not make much money, but I did get into a lot of trouble that day. The teacher did not think that selling was an appropriate activity to be conducting at school. Surprisingly, my parents were not mad; they just told me that business ventures would have to wait.

At sixteen, I was walking along the lakeshore, and I saw a large weathered stump that had washed ashore. To many, this was just an old rotted root, but I saw the potential in it. It was obvious. This stump could be made into a coffee table. Even though it was obvious to me of its potential, convincing others was much more difficult. It seems that no matter how good an idea is, others just do not see the genius.

The best way to view your budding entrepreneurship is to break it into four components: creativity, determination, risk, and luck. Each is equally important for success.

Creativity

Creativity is an intricate part of being a successful entrepreneur. The great ideas are out there; it just takes a different perspective to uncover them. Tap into your creative side. Sometimes, the stupidest ideas actually end up being the best. Creativity might actually be the hardest component to master. It is for me. When I was a child, my mother read to me or told me stories often. Once at the age of three, I came running to tell my father about the three bears and the funny things they were doing in our backyard. Dad did not think my story was funny and lectured me on being honest, but Mother saw my imagination at work and began to ask me more questions, showing enthusiasm as I continued. In a few moments with her encouragement, I had created my first story and personal version of the three bears. Perhaps it was at this early age of three that I grew to appreciate the imagination. In my business Waterwood Wonders, the driftwood I use to make my tables is not a material normally used to make tables. It takes creativity to see what others do not see.

Determination

Once you have your great idea, you must implement it, and to do so it takes a determined personality and faith in your idea to proceed. When people say, "We've never done it that way before," STOP and listen to their words. They may have never, but you are not them. When people say this, then this is when you know you are on the right track. In my business Waterwood Wonders, my friends did not see the beauty that lies at the root of each tree. They had never seen a table made of driftwood. They told me it would not work; however, I knew it would. After I had spent time shaping and forming my table, its beauty then became apparent to them. Sometimes, you have to go against what others say to follow your own vision. For any entrepreneur to be successful, you must have the support of family and friends, even if you have to encourage their support a little bit.

In a discussion with my mom, she expressed concerns about one of my business ideas. She holds great influence in my decision-making process, but I was determined that she was going to see it my way. That same day, we ordered Chinese food. While she was not looking, I took her fortune cookie and replaced it with a special cookie. Earlier, I had taken her cookie and carefully removed it from the wrapper. I took a pair of tweezers and removed the fortune from the cookie and replaced it with my own message. When she opened her cookie, it read: "Have faith in your sons and daughters." Suddenly, she was on board.

Risk

The single hardest part of starting a business is taking that first step, deciding that you are going to go forward with your idea, and working up the courage to dedicate yourself to the long road ahead. You are putting something at risk. To be successful, you must be comfortable with risk. Capital is needed to grow a business, and it can be difficult to risk your own money. Money is important, but I believe it can be dangerous to value money too extensively. Over-valuing money can cause you to turn down exciting business opportunities. When I was seventeen, I decided to start a pressure-washing business. In order to do this, I had to borrow one thousand dollars to purchase equipment. This was a big step for me. The risk paid off, and I was able to make enough to pay off my equipment within the first three months. On the flip side of risk comes responsibility. Be prepared to take responsibility for the actions of your company. My business Can Do Enterprises undertook a contract of pressure-washing asphalt. Though the company tried to do a good job, we did not have the expertise to satisfy the customer's needs. I had to take responsibility for the poor quality and did not charge the customer. That lesson cost me seventeen thousand dollars. In entrepreneurship, lessons can cost you tremendously. I have learned that by taking responsibility, your clients and customers will respect you more, and a relationship based on trust can be achieved.

Entrepreneurs have vision, yet you cannot be too proud to accept advice. People want to help you. They have been down this difficult road. By knowing their mistakes, you can ensure your success. It also helps to know what your skill set is. You cannot be an expert in every aspect of your business, so realize your strengths and exploit them. Minimize your weaknesses and concentrate your efforts into the areas where you'll succeed. For example, in an effort to save money, I decided to do my taxes myself. However, I figured my numbers wrong, and the mistake cost me twenty-six hundred dollars. Looking back on the situation, I should have hired a professional to do this for me. I am an expert at woodcarving, not at being a CPA.

Luck

Why some people have luck and others never seem to find it I don't know, but it's undeniable that some people are plain lucky. I have worked very hard for my accomplishments, yet often I feel that I am just the right person at the right time. Nevertheless, the key to luck is being prepared for situations at hand. Luck is having the confidence in yourself, in your business, and in your future. If you are prepared, then you CAN DO what it takes to become a successful entrepreneur.

Reaching Lofty Goals with Hard Work and Persistence

Michael Cain

Loft In Space

Northern Plains Region
Regional Partner:
University of Nebraska-Lincoln

Michael Cain

Michael Cain had the idea of starting Loft In Space during his freshman year at the University of Nebraska–Lincoln, where in the first year of business he sold sixty lofts to UNL students. The following year, he was able to double his sales by expanding to more schools in the area and improving his outreach to students who were arriving at UNL. Many of his college days have been spent getting involved in different student organizations, including Students in Free Enterprise, UNL Cornhusker Marching Band, and the Collegiate Entrepreneurs' Organization. With these experiences, Michael has grown and one day hopes to be the president and owner of a large national company. He is currently working at expanding Loft In Space to provide loft beds to many more students at other schools around the nation.

Loft In Space

FOUNDER:	Michael Cain
WEB:	loft-in-space.com
EMAIL:	mike@loft-in-space.com
PHONE:	402/610-2154
ADDRESS:	P.O. Box 776 Dakota City NE 68731

Mike's Bikes, Mike's Two-Way Radio, and Pure Excitement are all businesses that I had dreamed of owning when I was little. These life-defining dreams started when I was about four years old. I never knew what would come of these dreams, but I did know that I wanted to own a business. The requirements for my business were that it would be started and owned by me, and the business would be involved in something that interested me. These aspirations, combined with my parents' assistance, provided many opportunities to start small businesses.

My parents own a two-way radio business that used to be run out of our basement. One of the first things that I received twenty dollars for was to sew a couple of pairs of pants for business people whom my parents knew. The pants were sent to Minnesota and New Mexico. Sewing is one of the many talents that I have learned and have been able to use as a manufacturing process in other businesses.

When in elementary school, I had lemonade stand on my street corner. I had done the typical "boy summer jobs" like mowing lawns in junior high and high school. I had started to make stocking hats when in junior high also; this provided another opportunity for me to use my sewing skills to provide a product. All of these things were added into my regimen of school activities that required a lot of time, but the one thing that was constant throughout my involvement was my work ethic.

When high school started, it meant a whole new list of activities around the year. Fall, winter, spring, and summer all brought different activities for me to participate in. The biggest thing that I learned over this time period was that hard work paid off. The more work that you put in preparing, the less work you had to put in competing. The same can be applied to business; the more planning you do, the less stress you will have when a "situation" comes up.

Loft In Space is a very wonderful opportunity that came to me like an idea from the sky. I build loft beds for college dorm rooms. The chance to provide a loft for other fellow students interested me from the start because I enjoy building things and helping other people. This exceptional idea dropped onto me from space while living in a two-person dorm room as a freshman in college at the University of Nebraska at Lincoln (UNL). Space was hard to find, and we were getting tired of climbing over my things, so the answer for us was to build a loft for the room.

I spent a quite a bit of time planning how my loft would be built to be durable, unique, and comfortable. The University of Nebraska provided a metal frame that acts as the box spring for a bed. What most people do when building their loft is to put a piece of plywood on the top and just place the mattress on that. A down side for me was that I wanted a bed that would have a little bit more spring to it. My answer was to build a loft frame that was capable of holding the metal frame that the University gave us in the room. Another advantage to this was that I didn't have to store the bed frame in the basement of the dorm and worry about getting it back at the end of the year. With my plans in mind, I went home and went to work building my loft. Ten hours were spent the Saturday before Thanksgiving cutting, drilling, and assembling my bed. There was never any intention to do that again; I had a loft that would work for me the rest of my college stay. My opinion changed on this idea, however, when I started installing my loft.

While installing my loft in my dorm room, four neighbors came up to me and asked if I would build them lofts. Being a businessman, I quoted them a price and was asked to do the job for them. I spent a total of sixteen hours over the

Thanksgiving weekend building four lofts for my neighbors and then another four hours installing them on that Sunday. This is when my head started to turn: What if I advertise my lofts to other students? Could I make a business out of this and make some money? I was determined that I could, but I just needed to find the best way to go about finding the customers and getting my name out so that I could build the lofts in time to install them at the beginning of the fall semester. Questions needed answers, such as how to find any other information that would assist me in setting up Loft In Space. This involved speaking with many university officials to see if there was any way that I could use them to help my business grow.

The list of UNL officials is long. I had meetings with the dean of the college of business administration, the director of admissions, the director of new student enrollment, the director of housing, and even the chancellor of the university. Most of the people who spoke with me were very happy to hear that a student was starting a business and wanted to be successful. Speaking with these people helped me gain confidence on my ability to start a business. I encountered a few bumps in the road when meeting with the director of housing because he rents lofts to students who live in the dorms. However, I met with the UNL director of housing with intentions of trying to work with him. To help us both out, I explained what I wanted to do and what kind of information would be helpful.

When walking into the housing director's office (I'll refer to him as Dr. S), the first thing that he said was, "I have heard of you. The university lawyers called me to tell me about you and asked my position about it. I know what you are trying to do, and it isn't going to work." Shock immediately set in, but I managed to ask him why he thought my business was destined to fail since I was ready to do anything to make it succeed. Dr. S mentioned four things:

1. UNL didn't allow students to run a business out of their dorm room.

2. I couldn't use the phone that UNL provided.

3. No emails could be received to the email address that I was given by UNL.

4. Anyone who does work for UNL has to have a one million dollar liability insurance policy and a one million dollar insurance policy on any vehicle that is brought onto university property.

Dr. S advised me to drop the idea of starting a business and just take a part-time job like all the other college students. After giving his two cents, Dr. S figured that I would want to forget the whole idea and give up my dream of running my own business. I didn't like the idea of giving up that easily, and I didn't believe anyone should turn away from what he or she wants to do. With Dr. S right in my face telling me that I should quit, my reply was, "No, you just told me exactly what I needed to know. My next steps will be to get a post office box, a cell phone, a different email address, and then talk to an insurance agent." Dr. S was very impressed. The next twenty minutes in his office were spent answering his questions on why I responded the way I did and did not give up my idea. The meeting ended with his telling me that I was a very unique type of student. Now that I had my main competitor's support, I was encouraged to pursue the first year of my business.

My hard work continued with setting up the business and determining how I was going to reach my target market: incoming college freshmen. A friend from the University Marching Band who had expertise in designing advertisements and putting together a marketing plan offered to help me with all the things needed. Andy designed a wonderful brochure for me and also gave me a place to advertise my business during New Student Enrollment over the summer, when all new students and parents were on campus. The best way for people to see my product was via a loft model, built to scale. This model was put on display at a location that many of the people at New Student Enrollment would see, with brochures next to it. I had also tried to get a list of all the students who had applied to go to UNL that fall, but I found out via a letter from the UNL attorney that the list of names is not public information until the students register for classes. My time was spent finding a way to reach as many people as possible over the summer so that I could get all the lofts built for August. With my new brochure design and the New Student Enrollment booth, I was ready to start taking orders for the fall. I just didn't know yet how long it would take to get my first order.

With most of June gone, I didn't have more than five orders, and I was starting to worry that I might not be very successful in my business venture. In addition, I had not broken even with the brochure printing cost. Therefore, I attended some of the New Student Enrollment days to talk with parents and see what I could make happen. By the second week in July, more orders started to come in. It was always exciting to go to the mailbox and see how many would come that day. The record day for that summer was five, a feat that happened several times to my delight. Things were starting to look up for my Loft In Space. Customers were sending in orders with checks as payment to have a Loft In Space bed-frame built by me. It was a great feeling of success; I had been able to make work what some had said would not. It didn't matter how much money I made that summer. Happiness was found in the joy and triumph of starting a business.

Fifty-five orders were in and manufacturing had to begin, and with it a whole new list of problems arose. I designed a pattern to build the loft frames around. This cut down on the time it took to assemble the loft by eliminating any measuring. I also designed templates that could be laid on the end of the boards to mark-off where the holes would need to be drilled. These two things helped cut the building time down to about an hour a loft compared to four hours a loft that it took the first time. I and a couple of others worked for two weeks trying to get all the loft orders done in time to be installed during the first week of class. Building was going well, and I felt that we were right on schedule. Things got behind a little when an afternoon had to be taken off in order to find a truck to move all the lofts from Dakota City, where my parents live and have a workshop, to Lincoln, a 125-mile drive. This delay meant I had to stay up all night before my drive to Lincoln. I also had to schedule times to install the lofts in the dorm rooms of my customers.

Looking back on the process, installation was the hardest and most demanding part, not because the process of putting up a loft is hard, but because I was in the UNL marching band and had practice all day during the week before classes. The only free time I had was from about 11:30 A.M. to 1:00 P.M., 4:00 P.M. to 5:30 P.M., and after 10:00 P.M. until 8:00 the next morning. There were customers who were moving in during that week for things such as sorority rushes, athletic practices, and marching band rehearsals. Sacrifices had to be made, such as sleep and food. I think I ate a total of five meals that whole week and slept an average of four hours a night.

When it was all said and done for the first year of Loft In Space, I was pleased with the progress. Where many people would have given up, I stayed focused and determined to make my business a success. The persistence used to make this business grow will help me through many other difficulties. Never giving up on a dream is very important in life. If I had given up on the idea of Loft In Space, I don't know where I would be right now. Most likely I would be working at a part-time job that would not be nearly as rewarding as owning my own business. I encourage all of you to go for your dreams and never give up. If there is a bump in the road, such as my encounter with Dr. S, there will be some way to get around it. All that needs to happen is for you to have a dedication to your goal and a willingness to succeed in attaining that goal. Work hard at what you do, and you will prosper.

Building a Personal Brand: The Art of Obtaining Free Advertising and Promotion for Your Business

Kevin Colleran

BlabberForce Enterprises

New England Region
Regional Partner:
Worcester Polytechnic Region

Kevin Colleran

Kevin Colleran has been involved in online and offline business for over ten years. In addition to being named "North East College Entrepreneur of the Year," Kevin also received the national "College Entre-

preneur of The Year Award" by the College Television Network and was honored as one of the top "Youth Entrepreneurs of the Year" by the National Congress for Community Economic Development and the "Student Business Initiative Award" by Babson College. In 2001, Kevin was recognized by Ernst & Young as an honorary "Young Entrepreneur of the Year."

Kevin is a pioneer for young entrepreneurs and helps youth around the world start their own companies. *Entrepreneur* magazine has written a book featuring Kevin and other entrepreneurial teens called *How to Be a Teenage Millionaire*. He is the student founder of Babson College's first undergraduate incubator and is the co-CEO of Blabber-Force Enterprises, Inc., the first undergraduate business coming out of Babson. Kevin has been interviewed by *Newsweek, USA Today, Forbes, Inc.,* and numerous other magazines.

Colleran's current and previous business ventures include ClubVibes.com, Photo Masterpieces, Starting Page!, LiveService.com, and Cyber Marketing Solutions International. He was the special projects director and member of the board of directors for NEATO, the do-it-yourself media labeling company with over forty-five million dollars in sales.

BlabberForce Enterprises

FOUNDER: Kevin Colleran
WEB: blabberforce.com
EMAIL: kevin@kevcoll.com
PHONE: 617/290-8227

S tarting a business as a student is one of the most challenging, educational, stressful, and rewarding experiences a person can have in his or her life. Balancing school, work, and a social life while also trying to balance the checkbook and bank account can be an awesome responsibility, no matter how qualified a person may be. So, why do young entrepreneurs go through all of the trouble of starting their dream business now instead of waiting until after graduation? Many do it because of the amazing opportunities for free publicity and personal brand building!

Advertising and marketing costs can drain any company of its cash and be a huge stress factor for any CEO. All companies, no matter whether they sell products or services, are only valuable if customers are aware of what is being sold and how it can be purchased. Additionally, almost all young entrepreneurs will face discrimination and stereotypes due to their age, which must be overcome in order to remain successful in their business. It is up to the entrepreneurs to come up with unique and cost effective ways to get their name, face, and company out in the public for marketing and credibility purposes without breaking the bank in the process.

In recent years, there has been a big trend among all forms of major media to tell the story of young entrepreneurs and student CEOs. Entrepreneurship has become much more recognized and respected thanks to the days of dot-com millionaires. The general public has become fascinated to read and learn about the stories of these amazing young business people.

There are numerous opportunities for creative young entrepreneurs to capitalize on the public's fascination with entrepreneurship and student business owners by utilizing print, radio, Web, television, and other forms of media to promote themselves and their companies free of charge. By taking advantage of free publicity, young entrepreneurs can eliminate their marketing budgets and still feel comfortable with the fact that their businesses will receive plenty of exposure and brand awareness.

The following is a guide for young entrepreneurs to make themselves and their businesses worthy of receiving the amazing benefits of free publicity and market exposure.

Develop an Expertise

The first step for young entrepreneurs looking to reap the rewards of free publicity is to develop an expertise on a topic or subject related to the industry of their business. The rest of this chapter will explain the importance of this expertise and how it will be used to generate free publicity, but for now, it is important to learn how to recognize, research, and develop a specific expertise.

There are three important factors for any entrepreneur to consider when selecting his or her expertise:

First, the expertise must be something closely related to the business or industry in which the entrepreneur is focused. For example, with my college-marketing business Blabber-Force Enterprises, Inc., I decided that it was immensely important for me to become an expert in understanding the United States' college demographic and the various marketing techniques that have been implemented in an attempt to influence the college consumers. This expertise included a full understanding of who are typical college students, what they spend their money on, and what makes them purchase one product over a competing brand.

The second consideration for an entrepreneur to think about when selecting an expertise is to choose a topic that he or she is truly interested in. Just like in school, it is much easier for a person to learn about and master an interesting topic rather than something that is considered boring. This is an important factor because the entrepreneur will spend hundreds of hours researching and learning about the specific topic and must truly possess a passion in order to retain the information that is discovered and continue conducting more research. For example, I have always been interested in the entertainment industry and how companies use movies, television, and music to make their products stand out in the minds of young target consumers. I spent a great deal of time studying the different trends and strategies used by companies looking to tie their product to different entertainment mediums in order to gain brand awareness and appreciation. By my senior year of college, this interest and expertise in this type of marketing landed me a great consulting job working with some of the largest record labels in the world.

The third and final consideration for an entrepreneur when choosing an expertise is to focus on a topic that he or she is better positioned to master than other people with sim ilar businesses. This is important because an expert should have some kind of "inside track" to the topic that makes the entrepreneur more qualified than other experts in the same field. For me, it was a perfect match to become an expert on understanding the college demographic because I was also a full-time college student, which gave me an advantage over other older business owners claiming a similar expertise. No matter how much my competitors claimed they knew about the college market, none of them was actually part of the demographic like I was.

Once an entrepreneur has selected the most appropriate topic for him or her to research, it is important to gather knowledge on any and all aspects of the topic in order to become a legitimate expert. The entrepreneur must have a full working knowledge of all research, findings, statistics, facts, and other experts within the same field. This is not a one-time project; rather, becoming and remaining an expert requires constant reading and research to keep up to date on all information pertaining to the topic.

Media Fact Sheet

The media fact sheet is the most important aspect of any entrepreneur's quest to build a personal brand and obtain free advertising and promotion for his or her business. The media fact sheet can be related to a simplified one-page resumé that promotes all of the necessary information about the entrepreneur relevant for any media or press people interested in using the entrepreneur in a story, article, TV show, or radio program.

Structure of Media Fact Sheet

- Name and full contact information (address, email, phone, etc.)
- Description of expertise (as described above)
- List of potential interview topics
- Summary of awards and recognitions
- List of previous press coverage (publication, title of article, date of print)
- Mini-resumé (features quick descriptions of most important business accomplishments)
- List of possible interview questions (no more than 10)
- Personal quotes related to the topic of the article (makes it easier for journalists writing articles requiring quotes . . . and helps prevent embarrassing or incorrect misquotes)

Newspaper and Television News Coverage

Newspapers and television news reporters are usually overstressed due to their daily assignments and time-crunching deadlines. They are given a matter of hours to research, develop, write, and submit their stories to their editors, only to be given another assignment the very next day. As a result of their stress, newspaper and television reporters are usually eager to interview experts pertaining to their story immediately and do not have time for extensive research to find the very best people. Due to this quick turnaround, reporters usually quote the very first experts they can get in touch with and are grateful for any outside help they can receive for their story.

This immediate need and quick turnaround offers amazing opportunities for entrepreneurs looking to get free exposure in newspapers and television news. It is a priority for entrepreneurs to make sure that they are the first ones contacted by reporters covering stories that match their industry and expertise. In order to do this, entrepreneurs must approach the appropriate media persons well before the day that the news assignment is issued. This can be done by getting copies of newspapers and watching news coverage from as many media outlets as one can handle.

Entrepreneurs must take initiative by contacting specific reporters who write about topics pertaining to their industry and making the reporters aware of the entrepreneur and his or her specific expertise. This can be done through phone, email, or fax and should include a copy of the media fact sheet described above to be kept on file by the reporter for any future stories that require expert opinions and quotes.

Magazine Coverage

Unlike newspapers and television news, magazines usually finalize their content weeks before their issue date and assign stories to reporters well in advance. This allows reporters the ability to do much more thorough research and locate the most appropriate experts pertaining to their story. As with newspaper and television reports, entrepreneurs must personally contact reporters from magazines that cover news stories pertaining to their industry and expertise. Many magazines have databases of experts who can be used for specific stories, and it is important for entrepreneurs to make sure that their media fact sheet is on file and will be considered for upcoming stories.

Many magazines encourage their staff and freelance reporters to develop stories on their own and present them to the editors for consideration in upcoming issues. Because of this, many reporters are willing to listen to outside suggestions or "pitches" from people who have ideas for stories. This presents another great opportunity for entrepreneurs to develop a unique and interesting story about their life, business, or successes to present to reporters that may make for a potential feature story in the magazine.

Speaking Engagements

Literally thousands of conferences, trade shows, panels, and expos every year deal with nearly every industry and topic imaginable. Each of these events usually requires several experts and business professionals from within the specific industry to address the attendees in capacities ranging from panel discussions to keynote speeches. These events can be amazing opportunities for young entrepreneurs to gain recognition and credibility by presenting their story, insights, or ideas with the audiences. I have spoken around the world at conferences for young students, high school and college entrepreneurs, teachers, and even successful older entrepreneurs about my life story, struggles, and the lessons I have learned. These speaking engagements can instantly create a personal brand and company awareness among industry colleagues, suppliers, customers, and competitors. There is an implied expertise and credibility associated with people selected to speak at events such as these, which can do a great deal in moving a young entrepreneur into the spotlight of his or her industry.

Entrepreneurs can be selected to participate in these kinds of events by following many of the same techniques used to generate newspaper, magazine, and television exposure discussed previously. By utilizing simple Internet searches and queries of trade show databases, entrepreneurs can find event information and organizer contact information for those people who book the specific speakers. These organizers should be contacted similarly to magazine reporters and should be given a copy of the media fact sheet and samples of past speaking engagements. In some instances, organizers will request speaker proposals, which will require a summary of the speaker, topic to be covered, and benefit to the audience. The best part about speaking compared to print or television media, however, is that there is usually a salary or "honorarium" paid to each of the speakers in addition to coverage of all of the travel expenses incurred to attend the event.

There are unlimited possibilities for creative entrepreneurs to utilize personal and business branding and publicity to generate significant marketing exposure for products and services. The difficulties of being a young entrepreneur and having to deal with the stereotypes and glass ceilings that go along with being young can easily be overcome by positive media exposure and a recognized expertise. As long as the media trend of focusing on entrepreneurship continues, young people will be able to utilize their stories and business accomplishments to obtain valuable exposure that can be used for instant credibility. However, all entrepreneurs must take an active role and aggressively pursue the right people and opportunities in media to ensure that their company receives the valuable exposure rather than letting it go to the competition.

Packadorms— From Idea to Implementation

Matthew Fox
Packadorms

East Coast Region
Regional Partner:
Fairleigh Dickinson University

Matthew Fox

In 2001, Matthew Fox started Packadorms, LLC, a company that provides a comprehensive door-to-door summer storage service for college students. Packadorms distributes boxes and tape, picks up a student's belongings, stores them for the summer, and then delivers everything to the owner's new location the following fall. Packadorms has operated profitably since its inception. Currently, the company has increased its clientele by more than fifty percent.

Matthew graduated from Wesleyan University in Middletown, Connecticut, with a bachelor of arts degree in neuroscience and behavior. At Wesleyan, Matthew served in many roles. As a head resident for the Office of Residential Life, he managed six resident advisors who were responsible for two hundred students in three dormitories. A three-year member of student government, Matthew served as president of the student body, directed a student government that was autonomously responsible for allocating five hundred thousand dollars to student groups, made decisions related to social policy on campus, and represented student interests to the Wesleyan administration. Concurrently, Matthew successfully expanded his company to four schools in two states. After graduating in December 2002, Matthew joined a supply and distribution company in Cleveland, Ohio. Recently, Matthew has accepted a position with a hedge fund on Wall Street and plans to jump headfirst into the financial world. He will continue to operate Packadorms at select colleges and universities. Matthew's goal is to start new businesses after gaining additional experience working in industry.

Packadorms

FOUNDER: Matthew Fox
WEB: packadorms.com
ADDRESS: P.O. Box 2386
Middletown CT 06457

Anyone can start a company. In some states, it costs as little as two hundred fifty dollars to gain LLC (limited liability company) status and a federal tax ID number. The real challenge for you as an entrepreneur is to take your concept and turn it into a profitable venture. The key to being successful is not necessarily to invent a new item that the world has not yet seen. Instead, you want to be the best at something—anything—and find a way to earn money for your talent. My summer storage company, Packadorms, is not original in theory; people have been moving and storing their belongings for as long as transportation has been in existence. There are many important steps I have taken in order to turn my idea into a successful venture. I hope that by sharing how I approached the creative process and how I designed Packadorms, I will be able to assist you in starting your own business.

As background, I first incorporated Packadorms, LLC, when I was nineteen years old. I was sitting in my dorm room at Wesleyan University in Connecticut, thinking about different companies I could start. Initially, I was leaning toward starting a food delivery service. It was at this point that a senior approached me to discuss the lack of space for students to store their personal items over the summer. He thought I would be a good partner to try to help him resolve this problem. Several months later, he became overwhelmed by academic responsibilities, and I took on Packadorms while still only a concept and developed it into a business. I knew that many challenges lay ahead, so without any real experience, I was prepared to make some mistakes and approach this new challenge as a learning adventure. By taking the necessary steps and thinking through the obstacles I might face, I was able to create a company that turned a profit at Wesleyan in 2001 and then at four schools in two states in 2002.

Initial Concept

The first and most important thing you need to do is to simplify your initial concept. You must have one clear line of business and figure out how to be the best. This is vital to creating a sound business plan. Those individuals who fail to focus their vision never create even one useful product or service. For instance, in my business there are many options to expand my model. Do I want to store students' belongings over the summer? Do I want to ship their things home? Do I also want to rent them appliances during the school year and diversify my service model to include products? The decision I originally made was to streamline my process and store college students' belongings over the summer alone.

The next step is to seek advice and accept feedback from others who challenge your idea. People close to you will tell you that you cannot succeed for any number of reasons. My family, friends, and peers who were aware of my idea initially discouraged me. I was doing well academically, aligning myself to serve as the president of the student body as a junior, and enjoying my time as a "kid." My family felt that jumping into a new venture would detract from my other successes and that I should focus my attention toward my current challenges. If I had listened to their advice, Packadorms would not exist. I had to visualize my idea and be confident, or others would have easily dissuaded me from attaining my objective. It was imperative that I remain determined! When others offered constructive criticism, I judged their concerns seriously but dismissed general discouraging comments without a second thought.

Challenges

There are two general types of challenges you must consider. First, you must consider what obstacles serve as barriers to entry, and then you must address the operational challenges you will face while conducting business. At the beginning, I had to consider what challenges have prevented others from providing summer storage to college students. Furthermore, I had to ask myself difficult questions. Do I have the capital to start this business? Will this business interfere with my current employment or academic schedule? Do I have the contacts or advisors in my life whom I can rely on if I face problems? With Packadorms, I decided that I had the available resources necessary to succeed. At that point, I decided I was ready to start investing time and energy into my idea.

Next, you need to consider operational challenges. With Packadorms, I had to decide if it is possible to drive large trucks around a college campus that is overrun with traffic when students are leaving school. Can I really find trucks, labor, storage, insurance, and other inputs that I will need to make Packadorms work? Will people really pay for this service and if so, how much? Once I was able to reconcile these problems and potential obstacles, I was one step closer to starting my business.

Risk and Loss

This is not a complicated concept. You will need to decide what you are willing to lose in return for possible success. Risk can be broken up into two parts: deciding what risk you are willing to take and then deciding how you can limit your risk.

First, consider what you are willing to lose if everything falls apart. For instance, Packadorms appeared daunting when I first wrote down the risk on paper. What if the trucks crash and people die? What if boxes of students' belongings worth one million dollars-plus get damaged? These risk questions may sound rudimentary; however, they are vital to a business plan, and I had to seriously address my liability when I formed my company.

The next step is to decide how you can limit that risk. Will insurance cover everything? Can you organize your company under someone else's name with more financial strength? Would it be prudent to team up with someone else who is better suited to bear the responsibility? Would it be a smart move to create a structure where a partner would take on all the risk and then be rewarded without doing any real work? These are questions you need to consider. With Packadorms, I was not legally required to incorporate my concept and form a company to make money or store peoples' belongings. Simply paying taxes on the profits would have been enough. However, because I wanted to be conservative and insure everything, I made the decision to form a limited liability company. I know some risky people who have taken out fifteen credit cards, maxed them out, and then used that money to start their companies. Some have made millions; others are currently in debt. I feel individuals should choose their own path and satisfy their own comfort level.

Client Base

So, you think you have a great idea, but who will buy your product? Who will use your service? Even if you create an original item you think you will use every day of your life, will anyone else buy it? You need to determine who makes up your market. Your market consists of anyone and everyone who would consider using your product or service. For me, it included any student who was a freshman, sophomore, or junior. Therefore, it was important that I tailored my business model toward servicing these students' needs. For instance, Packadorms picks up students' belongings during their finals week. What about graduate students who have a finals week different from the rest of undergraduates? Is it financially rewarding to run extra trucks during the graduate students' finals week for ten more clients? In this case, I decided it was not financially rewarding to service this market. These are lessons I learned through trial and error. I had to understand my market before entering into my venture. I had to be sure not to speculate and expand my line of business during operations without serious thought, or else I would have weakened my overall concept.

Now that you understand your market, how do you refine your product or service? I had to consider many issues when designing Packadorms' trucking schedules. Is it better for students to have their belongings throughout their finals week so that they are not rushed to pack until their exams are over? Or will students prefer to give up their things so that summer storage concerns will not weigh on their minds during their finals schedule? For Packadorms, instead of trying to dictate to my clients based on my personal preference (to coordinate my storage before taking my finals), I decided to allow them to choose their pickup time by giving them several options during finals week. Also, I invested more money into my company to accept credit cards in the second and third years because I found that credit card acceptance improved the ease of service. This helped increase my number of patrons because students do not want to take time and effort to address a letter and send a check. Additionally, parents often pay for the service, and credit card acceptance enables them to complete the transaction online in one smooth step.

Selling Points

How will you sell your idea? Are you the only company providing a product or service? Do you have a unique advantage over your competitors? Are you cheaper? I needed to decide what selling points Packadorms would have that I could convey to my market. Once I surveyed the current storage options available at Wesleyan University in 2001 and realized that they would not solve the problems of all students, I knew I would be able to create a successful service. For my company, I felt that we had reasonable prices and great service.

The most obvious way to appeal to an individual is to tell them that you will save them money. I analyzed the price it would cost to store students' belongings based on the cost of renting storage space. I felt that by making my cost below that point, I would be able to drive home the worth of my service. Moreover, it is less expensive to use our service than to use any other option. We provide a quality service for less money; who can argue with that!

After I convey to the student and parent that Packadorms is less expensive than doing it yourself, I continue to drive home the convenience factor. Our entire service is door-to-door. We drop off boxes, pick up peoples' belongings, and then return them at the start of the fall semester. Our system enables students to use our service without ever stepping outside their dorm rooms! Any business can be successful if it has one selling point. Once I was able to clearly classify and convey the advantages my business offers to my customers, I was ready to decide how to market my company.

Marketing

To choose how to market is a true economic challenge for a small business. First, you will need to decide how much you are willing to spend, and then you will need to decide how to advertise. Choose your spending limit based on your previous decisions about risk. If you are willing to accept losing more money, then spend more on advertising. With Packadorms, I was not willing to spend much money on advertising. Once I determined how much I was willing to spend on marketing, I was ready to choose my marketing methods.

You have already identified your clientele, learned how to structure your business to best suit their needs, and finalized the amount of money you will invest in your marketing efforts. It is now time to choose how to advertise. In order to get the word out about your product or service without breaking the bank, you will have to be thrifty. With Packadorms, I realized I was dealing with a college campus, and I could get away with minimizing cost. Flyers on fluorescent paper stand out, and while a temporary eyesore on a pristine campus, they serve their purpose in drawing attention toward my business. Additionally, people put flyers in the worst possible locations, such as on bulletin boards. Therefore, I was very successful in marketing by handing out flyers at dining halls and outside of dormitories. Packadorms has successfully built a brand name at schools without investing heavily in newspapers, radio stations, or painted company cars with bullhorns. Again, I was successful because I thought deeply about my market and how I would attract potential clients to use my company before I spent my first dime on advertising.

Partners

This is the last topic in this passage, and without question, the most important. Remember, partners are not always necessary, but they are often a good idea. People frequently think that when they are looking for business partners, they should look for people with experience. Most entrepreneurs believe that they are talented and if they can get people with real-world knowledge or training "on-board," their mission will succeed. This is not the case. There are two main traits you should look for when choosing a business partner: loyalty and previous success.

First, you must work with someone you can trust. Take out a blank piece of paper and write down ten people who, if your car broke down at 2:00 A.M., would pick you up without question. Initially, I teamed up with smart people whom I met through family or friends. After the first year of operation, I was let down by some of these people. They did not come to me with their problems. Instead, they were not honest with me, and the business faltered. Without trust, I was always uneasy, and I wondered if my instructions and plans were being followed.

Next, you should look for someone who has been successful in any field or activity. Similar to the way employers value young people who have experience competing athletically or debating scholastically, you should look for people who know not only how to win but how to go for a goal and fail. Choosing a business partner or teammate who does not possess both loyalty and aptitude will hurt your ability to successfully manage and grow your company. With Packadorms, I chose to work with people who had been successful in any field. Some had excelled in debate, others in athletics. I find it is important to surround yourself with successful individuals because they are the people who will be able to meet new challenges when they arise.

I encourage you to consider the steps that I took with Packadorms, LLC. I hope you will be able to apply the guidelines I used to your own brilliant idea. Remember, do not be afraid to ask for help along the way and be sure to thank all of those people who have been instrumental in your success. Without my parents, Michael and Vicki; my business partner, Bethany Goughenour; and my friends and family, I would not have been able to create my company.

I wish you the best of luck in all of your future endeavors. Be confident when you set your goals and work hard to achieve them. Though it is important to achieve success and make money, be sure to enjoy the journey.

In Search of Success

Alberto Garza Vázquez
ZABERICA

Mexico Region
Regional Partner:
Instituto Tecnológico y de Estudios
Superiores de Monterrey Campus

Alberto Garza Vázquez

Alberto L. Garza Vázquez was born in Tampico Tamaulipas, Mexico, in 1974 where he lived with his mother, Clara Irma Vázquez, and his sisters, Karla and Fabiola Garza Vázquez, until he was twenty-three years old. He was studying college-level engineering and agronomics in Tampico when he decided to make a change and move to Monterrey, Nuevo Leon to study international commerce, specifically agribusiness, at the Instituto Tecnologico y de Estudios Superiores de Monterrey. During this time, he had two businesses running successfully. The first one, ZABERICA, provided greater value for lower costs. Some of the products Vázquez managed were pickled hot peppers and hot sauce. The company harvested the product from the Tamaulipas agricultural field in a local plant. His second company, Industrial Structures and Designs, was established to collaborate with another company, Lonas Jiménez, which manufactured canvases. The two companies together were able to have a greater market: Industrial Structures and Designs created awnings with a metallic structure that could then be covered with canvas. Presently, the company continues to work in collaboration with Lonas Jiménez but has extended its products to include new markets, such as the soft drink, car, and steel industries in the industrial sector of the northern part of Mexico.

ZABERICA

FOUNDER: Alberto Garza Vázquez
PHONE: 83-87-00-81
ADDRESS: Maria Curie #532A, Col. Roma
Monterrey, N.L. Mexico

Sometimes, we might ask ourselves what is success. Success is defined in the *Longman Dictionary of American English* as "to gain a purpose or reach an aim." However, in real life, people may have a different perception of success based on their personal experiences and thoughts. I define success as a personal strength that motivates you to obtain things, to make all of your dreams come true, and to reach your personal and professional goals.

Our lives are always full of challenges and various obstacles that we have to confront bravely. These challenges are a way of motivating ourselves to fight and continue, to be able to obtain things that we have not even dreamed or thought of. I think that the majority of successful entrepreneurs are those individuals who have reached their hopes, goals, and dreams through fighting hard to be who they are now and for what they have. I think that when an easy course is presented to us, we take it without even thinking, but when we do not have the means of obtaining things easily, we discover inner strength and integrity.

I am one of those people who has lived day after day with the fighting, dreaming, and encouraging spirit. As a child, I lost my father's financial and emotional support because my parents got a divorce, but instead of crying all day over the many difficulties, I chose to look into the future and to work for a better life for myself and for my community. The absence of economic resources forced me to work harder to obtain basic things, such as my studies and personal necessities.

I live in Mexico, and in my country, studying in a public or in a private university makes a big and noted difference. I lived my childhood in a public school where I made a lot of "business" in terms of my own possibilities. For example, when I was in third grade, I spent a lot of time selling popcorn during the school breaks and painting desks during vacations. I did everything I could in my spare time to make money to pay for my books and rides on the school bus. In those moments, my fighting spirit was born.

Ever since I was a little, I learned to be proactive, to look for opportunities in my environment, and to try to be something more. The years went on and I understood that to be successful is not easy; generally, we have to spend a lot of time trying hard to get what we want to obtain. This is why we have to believe in ourselves and is why I decided to believe in myself from the start.

After I finished my basic studies, I enrolled in two technical high schools, an electromechanic and an automotive mechanical high school. Since I was a child, I had to work to pay my school expenses, including elementary and technical schools. By this time, I didn't have the financial security to go to college, but my desire to be a successful professional made me join to the agronomic engineer career track in the Universidad Tecnológica de Tamaulipas, where I eventually was elected as the Student Society president. During this period, the students that lived in the State of Tamaulipas attended an Agribusiness Congress organized by the Instituto Tecnológico y de Estudios Superiores de Monterrey (ITESM). The students who did not have the necessary economic resources to travel were given a scholarship. Generating those scholarships involved us in different tasks, such as selling camp products, obtaining Tamaulipas government and private enterprise sponsorships, and organizing several activities with the students under my leadership.

During that congress held in Monterrey city, I met the career director, who is the person in charge to coordinate and administrate the agribusiness area. I talked with him about all the activities and efforts involved with our participation in the ITESM Congress as well as the importance of our being there. When he discovered that I was the group leader, he invited me to join the ITESM. Previously, I never thought I would be able to finish my career at ITESM because of my limited economic capacity, but I considered my education at this new institution a challenge, and some months later I made it. I found myself studying at ITESM, leaving behind three years of study in the State of Tamaulipas but with a new and growing hope. I combined my studies and my hard work to reach my new dream.

When I was in fifth semester of my agribusiness studies, I also had the opportunity to participate in the Entrepreneur Program where I developed a project focus in the camp, which consisted of industrializing agricultural products in order to generate more income for farm workers. This project lead me to the North American International Award 2002 in Mexico. This was a very important experience in my agribusiness career because I saw that my work was recognized.

I started my studies without knowing with what economic resources I would be able to finish them. Today, days apart of accomplishing this dream, I can happily note the great value of my perseverance and efforts. I had obtained a scholarship of forty-five percent, and concurrently I had worked to pay the rest of my tuition. It had not been easy, but I had worked very hard in that aspect. I started working in a canvas company named Lonas Jiménez, S.A. de C.V., where I worked on a very important project fabricating metallic structures. We helped the company to diversify the products that it offered and increased its sales growth by sixty percent in just one year.

Simultaneously, I began a vegetable industrialization project in the State of Tamaulipas. This project consisted in developing field products from their selection, processing, formulas, packaging, and brand development to its commercialization and marketing. Everything was combined with various rural workers, who obtain economic benefits by placing their product on the market with a better price and better quality.

I currently see the Mexican camp as an opportunity area in which we, the entrepreneurs, can make a lot of business, satisfy the market, and, at the same time, accomplish integral development to the rural families—because if the rural workers obtain a better salary, then they can increase their quality of life. I think that it is also important to integrate the women and children into the productive process, allowing the families to have greater incomes. Whereas the men work in the crops, the women can work in the industrialization processes like product selection, packaging, etc., and children can perform simple tasks to help their mothers. In turn, the women can teach their children to be successful entrepreneurs in their communities and to grow up working hard to make their dreams come true.

These two activities, the fabrication of metallic structures and the plan for the Mexican field, lead me to condense the project that took me to the North American International Awards 2002 in Mexico. This award is a way to recognize entrepreneurial efforts of trying to be a better person and overcoming difficulties. It is also a way of motivating and confirming that I can get whatever I have in mind with my dedication and perseverance. I invite you to follow your dreams and to make a difference in the world.

It is very important always to have burning the entrepreneur spirit. You need motivation that moves you to distinguish yourself above others, leads you to risk everything that you have following your dream, and allows you to accomplish your goals. For example, when the ITESM published the call to participate in the North American International Award

2002, together with other entrepreneurs I took the decision to register in the competition. Different from the other students, I worked hard on the presentation of the project to be the best and to get the award. I feel a great satisfaction because I accomplished my goal and brought the award to Mexico.

Today I feel proud of my job; however, I know that I can always give more and I can always be a better person. Here are some words of wisdom I have learned that all successful entrepreneurs possess:

● There is always hope, even though the road seems very rough and complicated.

● We are always capable of discovering more strength in ourselves to resolve all difficulties that life presents.

● The honesty and the hard work dignify and produce good changes that lead us to obtain all of what we desire and dream of.

● Asking is not a sign of weakness, but rather it is a sign of the determination that we have inside ourselves to make our dreams come true.

● The adversities should not be considered problems but instead as opportunities to discover our virtues and capacities.

● In life there are not ends; there are always new things to accomplish and more dreams to make come true.

Being a student helps young entrepreneurs in the following ways:

● Education is the best way that we have to convert our professional goals into reality.

● We must be full of integrity, both professionally and personally.

● We should praise the people we work with and listen to the opinions of our coworkers and families.

● It is best to resolve complicated situations with fewer

resources but with more efficiency.

● Successes and failures obtained during our student lives are the result of individual efforts. We should demand more of ourselves each day.

● Every student who desires to overcome obstacles has the right of doing it by the means of formal education.

Being an entrepreneur has taught me that:

● We all have creative capacities, but it is only the determination that matters.

● Success depends on the effort and time that we are willing to dedicate to our dreams.

● It is never too late to reach our goals.

It is not an easy task to accomplish our personal goals; however, it is not impossible. I consider myself like a professional change agent in my environment and in my society. Entrepreneurs are great dreamers; we have to fight for what we want, giving more of ourselves. This includes not saying "I can't" or "I don't know." Only if we work for success day after day, can we become better entrepreneurs today and tomorrow.

When Life Gives You a Lemon, Make Lemonade

Lance Larson
OC Hosting

Southwestern Region
Regional Partner:
Loyola Marymount University

Lance Larson

Lance Larson is a 21-year-old full-time senior studying information and decision systems at San Diego State University in southern California. Now a senior at SDSU, Lance is currently the RCA computer technician for his dorm. In 2002, he was named Entrepreneur of the Year for the Southwestern Region of the Global Student Entrepreneur Competition.

While attending SDSU, Lance also attended the Reserve Police Academy in San Diego, graduating with top honors. As a reserve police officer for the city of Laguna Beach, California, he was presented the Medal of Life Saving in October 2001.

Lance's entrepreneurial efforts began at age fourteen, when he ventured into his first real business, South Coast Computing, which offered networking services and computer repairs. From that experience grew his current business, OC Hosting, Inc., a corporation offering high-speed Internet access, advanced web hosting, and dedicated server solutions to over two thousand customers worldwide. Lance has become a Comp TIA Inet+ Internet Subject Matter Expert and has helped develop security systems and Internet certification tests. He is also a graduate of the Cisco Internet-working Academy and has Computer Repair/A+ Certification.

In 2003, Lance was accepted as an FBI Honors Intern with the Federal Bureau of Investigation in Quantico, Virginia, in the FBI Computer Forensics Laboratory. After that, he will operate his business while finishing his MBA. His goal is to expand OC Hosting, Inc., into the world's largest web-hosting provider.

OC Hosting

FOUNDER:	Lance Larson
WEB:	OChosting.com
EMAIL:	lance@ochosting.com
PHONE:	888/909-4678
ADDRESS:	P.O. BOX 772 San Clemente CA 92674

At age four, all I wanted to do was eat cereal and watch cartoons. At nine, it was candy and friends to ride bikes with me. But by eighteen, my interests had changed dramatically—I owned and operated a corporation that was grossing four hundred thousand dollars per year and serving over two thousand clients in fifty-two countries, twenty-four hours a day, seven days a week, 365 days a year. It sure beat flipping burgers at McDonald's! Here's what happened in those "wonder years" between nine and eighteen.

I grew up in beautiful San Clemente, a small beach town located along the sprawling Southern California coastline. While growing up, I had a paper route, performed odd jobs around my neighborhood, and surfed the waves up and down the coast. It was the typical lifestyle of a southern Californian teenager. There was, however, one thing about me that was different from others my age—I had a thirst for success and an overwhelming need to explore new endeavors.

When I was nine, I came up with the idea to try selling lemonade. I enlisted my friend and new "business partner" Damian Cappel, and together we set up a neighborhood stand. The lemonade business was best during hot summer days when surfers, tourists, and other beach-goers passed by our house on their way to the cool ocean waters just at the end of our street. And a good many of our customers were people I knew from my paper route or kind neighbors who were coerced into buying a fifty-cent glass of ice-cold lemonade. I learned about timing, location, and public relations at an early age.

During the lemonade stand's first year, Damian and I handpicked lemons from neighborhood trees. We spent hours squeezing and combining our "special" ingredients to make the perfect lemonade concoction. As our little business grew, there were times when we couldn't meet the demand for our fresh-squeezed juice. So rather than lose sales, a little Crystal Light powder became one of our "special" ingredients. Before long, we diversified and started selling cookies, milk, and hot chocolate during the colder summer days when our lemonade sales were down. Our typical day's profit was ten dollars, which we split evenly at the end of each day. I learned to make sure that I had a desirable product to deliver, looked for ways to diversify, and tried to always be fair in my business dealings.

Toward the end of one afternoon, Damian and I were sitting at our lemonade stand, waiting for a few last customers before we packed up. Two surfers in their early twenties pulled up to our stand in a small black pick-up truck with wetsuits hanging out the back. The passenger got out and asked how much we wanted for a glass of lemonade. Damian told him we were out of our large cups, and all we had left was a small size for fifteen cents. The next thing we knew, the surfer grabbed for our money box—which had been lying in plain view on the table and contained our meager ten dollars in change and bills—quickly jumped back into the truck, and the driver peeled out.

We sat there for a moment, stunned and devastated. We couldn't believe that we'd been robbed—right in front of my house, in the idyllic neighborhood we'd grown up in! At nine years of age, we didn't realize that people like those men existed. We waited there for twenty minutes, thinking they'd come back and say "just kidding," give back our moneybox, and buy a few glasses of ice-cold lemonade. Boy, were we wrong . . . and disappointed. We finally went in the house and told my mom. She called the San Clemente Police Department, which sent two squad cars to search our neighborhood for the two lemonade bandits. (They were never found.)

Somehow, a local newspaper reporter heard about the

incident and asked if he could interview us for an article. It must have been a slow weekend for news because our story not only made the headlines in our local paper but also drew the interest of most of the major television news channels. About six television crews—ranging from ABC to the "Barbara Walters Show"—showed up the next day. They waited in line at our lemonade stand for interviews with Damian, my mom, and me. Needless to say, we sold a lot of cookies and lemonade—most of it mixed with Crystal Light—that day.

By the time all the commotion of scheduling, media interviews, and lemonade sales were finally over, we ended up with over three hundred fifty dollars in cash donations, a huge box of baseball cards, a deluxe new stand-up sign that read "Ice-Cold Fresh Lemonade," and many other generous gifts. We donated most of the money, acting on the advice of our mothers, to Greenpeace and The Surfrider Foundation. And I learned that business can bring tough times, but if you can overcome the experience, you'll reap rewards. This is when you get to drink the lemonade.

By the seventh grade, running a lemonade stand wasn't such a "cool thing," so I set out to find something new. My school had a computer lab that was open every day during lunch. I didn't know as much about computers or the Internet as I wanted to, so I decided to spend my lunchtime in the lab. The school's technology director, Mrs. Ozonian, was patient enough to answer my daily barrage of questions, while making sure I didn't blow up anything. By the summer of my seventh-grade year, she offered me a job as a network engineer, working on the school's computer network for $4.25 an hour. I enthusiastically accepted and set out to learn as much as I could.

I gained invaluable experience that summer and began building my resumé—one of the most important documents you can have for future employment. I discovered how innovative information technology was and realized I didn't want the boat to sail without me. I decided to open my own computer repair business, South Coast Computing. I was such a sponge for new information that I offered on-site computer repair service—free of charge. However, I soon discovered that I could create a profitable business from my "hobby" while doing something I considered fun and exciting. I began charging $25 an hour to friends and relatives, but they all told me I wasn't charging enough. So I listened to my customers and happily raised my rates to $65 an hour, then $85 an hour, and my customers still paid me—and called me back!

I soon discovered that running a business at the age of fifteen would be quite a challenge. I remember when I went to meet my first business customer. I wore a polo shirt and a nice pair of slacks (which I had to borrow from a next-door neighbor). When I walked in the door with my briefcase and computer toolkit, I was met with a very surprised look. I could tell the client was thinking "Where's your dad, kid?" as I shook his hand, introduced myself, and told him I was there to help. The most interesting thing was that almost every client I met for the first time had this very same reaction—until I sat down at their computer system and fixed one problem after another. This made me realize that instead of thinking that we're at a disadvantage being young entrepreneurs, I think we've actually been presented with one of the greatest business opportunities we could ever wish for. How so? Because those who succeed in business at a young age have an even better chance to succeed in life.

Young people in business do, however, have to face more obstacles than their older counterparts. We're not considered to be great thinkers due to our lack of life experience. The hardships I faced as a young person starting a business were an uphill battle, and that made me try harder. I scouted the market to determine how and where I should/would offer services. I picked a business name and obtained a business license. I made business cards and flyers. I started telling family, friends, and my contacts in the community about my business. I placed an ad in the Yellow Pages of the community phone book. And my business rapidly expanded.

I gradually shifted my focus from computer repair to designing websites. My computer clients had started asking me to do more than just repair work. They wanted me to design and manage the hosting of their websites. As I designed more and more websites, I began to recognize a problem in the industry—there were no inexpensive, reliable website hosting providers. (Note: Website hosting is the storage of your company's website on a very large computer system, which is connected to very fast Internet lines twenty-four hours a day. A "web host" is responsible for sending a copy of your website to whoever requests to see it.) I thought I could fill this spot. My technical knowledge, combined with my desire to build my business by doing most of the work myself, allowed me to charge less than some of the big companies. So I began my largest business venture yet.

The doors of Orange County Hosting opened in April 2001. It was funded with money I had saved from all my previous jobs. At first, I only operated with two web-serving computers and about fifty clients. My aim was to serve local clients, but I was amazed when the first order I received was from Europe. I quickly decided to change the company name from Orange County Hosting to OC Hosting, to create an image that my business was larger than it actually was. But the truth was, I was running the business from my bedroom floor, and as clients started to pour in from around the globe, I needed help—and a better office.

So, I set out to find employees, office space, and a bank

account. I quickly discovered that if you're under eighteen, most banks will require a parent to co-sign when you open a bank account. And that means your mom or dad becomes responsible for your liabilities. I decided I didn't want the person who did my laundry each week to be in any legal trouble. But as a budding entrepreneur, I didn't have a lawyer. All it took, though, was my first court case against a client who wouldn't pay his bill, and I decided I better have legal protection. I found a lawyer who charged me one thousand dollars to incorporate OC Hosting. That meant that OC Hosting, Inc., became its own entity with its own bank account, tax liabilities, and its own group of officers—all of whom can run and manage the company without fear of being personally sued.

Next, with bank account in hand, I started looking for an office. Almost every property manager I encountered ran a credit check. But since I was young and didn't have any credit, I was turned down for four different office spaces. Then, I found a privately owned office building, which meant I could deal directly with the building's owner instead of a property-management company. I met with the owner and presented him with personal, financial, and reference information. I showed him newspaper articles about me and my business and a letter from my bank. I went into that meeting with the attitude that I had to "sell myself" to the owner. Apparently I did pretty well as OC Hosting had its own office space the next day.

With office space leased, I needed to hire a few employees. I've always believed that friends make the best employees. You already know you can get along, so it shouldn't be much harder to tolerate them as employees. I approached several friends from high school and asked if they would like to work with me, in furthering my ideas and adding their own. I've learned that if I work for my employees, they'll work for me. They're my bosses—they dictate how I handle situations and conflicts. Two friends who played football with me in high school agreed to come into the business. They were excited to be part of a new Web-hosting business.

Today, OC Hosting, Inc. operates with ten full-time employees, over two thousand clients, a 1,400-square-foot Network Operations Center, and over fifty thousand dollars in revenue per month. We offer a full range of services, including dial-up Internet connections, high-speed wireless Internet, domain-name registration, and, of course, website hosting. We even provide services to such high-profile websites as **Billyidol.com** (the official Billy Idol website). OC Hosting's customer-first approach and its ability to quickly adapt to industry changes has kept the business profitable and made it a major industry competitor.

As young entrepreneurs, we're given the gift of time, unlimited education, an extensive potential client base, and the ability to turn boundless ideas into profitable businesses. In high school, I played sports, ran a business, and spent time with friends. High school provides an infinite source of business ideas and potential clients.

I've had the privilege of meeting a few other young entrepreneurs who started their businesses while in school, servicing their classmates. For example, Phil Dade raised five hundred thousand dollars from investors while in high school and created a website for students interested in practicing for college Advanced Placement tests; Tolga Tarhan started a website design business when he was in high school and sold it for one million dollars; Robert Maynard started an Internet service provider, **Ojai.net**, while a freshman in high school.

The number of potential businesses you can start during your school years is unlimited. You could consider a gardening service, pet-care business, class note-taking service; obtain a resale license so you can sell various products; or turn your hobby into a business. And remember: happy customers are the best advertisement!

Transforming Work into Fun and Your Fun into Money!

Daniel Murza

Sandow SK Classic

East Coast Region
Regional Partner: Canadian
Council for Small Business
and Entrepreneurship

Daniel Murza

Born May 3, 1980, Daniel Richard Murza grew up in Saskatoon, Saskatchewan, Canada—right in the middle of hockey country. The youngest of three children, he grew up playing many different competitive sports, including hockey, soccer, and tennis. He played soccer for the University of Saskatchewan men's soccer team and was a first-team Academic All-Canadian during his time with the Huskies. He finished his university career in May 2003 after completing his bachelor of commerce degree with great distinction and majors in finance and business economics. Despite his passion for the sport of soccer, it was his interest in hockey that sparked the idea for his business venture, Sandow SK Classic, which has its own line of replica hockey jerseys of past eras.

Murza's business successes have earned him several awards, including first place in University of Nebraska's Donald Duncan/Duncan Aviation and Queen's University's International Business Plan competitions, the Queen's Gold Medal for entrepreneurial excellence, the Raj Manek Memorial Prize in Entrepreneurship, and the 2002 Canadian Collegiate Entrepreneur Award, which is sponsored by the Canadian Council for Small Business Management and Entrepreneurship. The media have recognized his accomplishments through various newspaper articles, television spots, and magazine articles. His media spots have made him a spokesperson for young entrepreneurs as well as local economic development in his province.

Sandow SK Classic

FOUNDER: Daniel Murza
WEB: sandowsk.com
EMAIL: info@sandowsk.com
PHONE: 306/341-0830

For me, student life has been an amazing adventure, full of excitement and free from the unwanted stresses and monotony of a nine-to-five workday. Depending on the area of study, a student's workload can be much less strenuous than that of most careers; on top of that, students have the time to go out almost every night with friends and sleep in the next day. Unfortunately, student life does eventually come to an end, and the dreaded career that will last the next thirty or forty years of your life lies ahead. Without even mentioning the tediousness of a job search, the prospects of a career that you settle for rather than choose is not too appealing.

Finding Your Dream Job

What if you could get up in the morning without slamming the snooze button ten times because you are excited about the new workday? What if the "workday" didn't even seem like work at all? There may be some dream jobs out there that would get you up in the morning, but those are few and far between, and the people who have them are probably not too keen about giving them up. So, why not make up a dream job for yourself?

The thought of creating your own job probably doesn't even enter the minds of a lot of students, but it did for me. This seems like a big endeavor, but if you start small and do something you are passionate about and interested in, it isn't as risky as it seems. This is exactly what I did—I started small by developing a hobby into a business. Everyone has a hobby of some sort. Whether it is website creation or even watching movies, there are business opportunities in virtually everything. A Web design company is an obvious entrepreneurial venture for someone who loves to make websites, but the movie enthusiast has opportunities as well. He or she could open a video store or even write a book with movie reviews. For me, my passion is sports, and my hobbies have included collecting sports memorabilia and even simply watching sports on television.

Developing Your Hobby into a Business

It may feel like a stretch to develop your hobby into a business, but if you start now, there is very minimal risk involved since you don't have much to lose. Starting small will get your feet wet to see what works and what doesn't work before you dive into investing a lot of money into creating a career for yourself. My experience is a perfect example of starting small when developing a hobby into a business.

My business venture started as a second-year university student. At the time, I was getting interested and somewhat "hooked" on eBay (**www.ebay.com**), an online auction site that hosts auctions for almost everything imaginable. This was about the same time that the New York Giants had just made the Super Bowl, and the hype around the team was enormous. It just so happened that I had an old Giants football jersey that I had never worn, and it had been sitting in my closet collecting dust for years. This was my chance to experiment with eBay and maybe make a bit of money. I borrowed my grandfather's Polaroid camera and took a couple snapshots of the jersey to list it on eBay during Super Bowl week. The response was phenomenal, and I sold the jersey for more than ten times what I paid for it!

After my first profitable sale and an enjoyable eBay experience, I immediately scrounged around my house for other items I could sell. I eventually found an old hockey jersey of the Soviet Union that I had purchased at a local store some ten years ago when I was not only a hockey fan but a hockey player as well. I remembered that the store had a huge stock of older jerseys that would be quite popular to hockey fans and collectors online since most of them are no longer produced. I had no money to buy a stock of them for resale, so I made an agreement with the store manager, who allowed me to purchase the jerseys in single quantities at bulk prices. This also allowed me to sell them on eBay and then purchase them from the store and send them off once I received payment from the eBay customer. This way, I didn't need a penny to make a business venture out of my hobby!

Although you may not necessarily find an opportunity similar to this one related to your hobby, there are still dozens of ways to start small. If you love movies, why not make an arrangement with a local movie store to sell their previously viewed movies over the Internet? You could also attach a personal movie review and rating to each movie you sell and include it with product descriptions on your website. Buyers with large movie collections would love to have reviews of each of their movies to show guests when picking out a movie to watch. This could also create a following of repeat customers for yourself if they enjoy your reviews. Commission from these sales may not yet be able to cover all of your bills, but this can supplement a full-time job or even full-time studies until you expand enough to make it your career. I was a student while I was selling the stock from the local hockey shop online, so the money simply helped pay tuition and a couple of nights out on the weekend.

The benefit of doing something you enjoy is that you already have the necessary base of knowledge required to make the initial sales. In essence, you are an expert at your hobby. Just as I knew which hockey teams were popular and which jerseys would sell well during given months, you know which movies to purchase for resale and when to push the sales of each one. Once you have enjoyed success with your initial venture, much of the risk of expanding will disappear since you now have knowledge of not only your hobby and pastime but also of the marketplace that promotes it. This knowledge will help you pick and choose which expansions or new products would be successful in such a market place. However, there is still some risk as expanding, usually requires financing. The best way to handle the new risk is to make a business plan now while you are starting small.

Expanding Your Business

Expansion can be as simple as selling movie posters as well or can be as large as opening an independent video store. The next stage for the expansion of my business was to begin to produce my own brand of jerseys under my new company name, Sandow SK Classic. Sandow is a former company that used to produce jerseys many famous hockey players once wore, including the likes of Wayne Gretzky and Bobby Orr. I re-trademarked the name to recreate a "classic" rendition of the now "classic" sportswear. Since creating my own brand of jerseys required more than just the change found in the couch cushions and in my winter jacket, I created a business plan in a university entrepreneurship class. My plan ended up being very promising and won several collegiate business plan competitions. A business plan not only maps out your expansion, but it also can help secure financing with investors. Mine was able to secure financing from a local bank due to its success in competitions. Not everyone has the advantage of an entrepreneurship class to make a fine-tuned business plan, but that isn't the only way to get help with a plan. There are many other people and organizations that can help. If you are a university student, there are likely several business faculty members at your school who would be glad to help. Many universities also have entrepreneurship and career centers that can help. Governments are always pushing for new business development, especially by young people, so they sponsor a lot of business creation and mentorship programs as well. If it is a very small venture that you don't want to spend much time on, you can always purchase a book or get reference material off the Internet on creating business plans. Once you have created your business plan, the next step is to implement the plan.

Recently, I have started to implement my plan, which entails many years of designed expansion. I have already created a product line of old-style hockey jerseys of various rare and defunct teams and am working on a clothing line that matches that same era of sports. There are still many more large steps in expanding, including wholesaling to retail stores and pursuing appropriate licensing. These are very big goals, and I must keep working on smaller steps to expansion before I can really go after them. Now that I have more advanced marketplace knowledge, I can start to add other items to my product mix using the research I did in making my business plan. Just as I can easily add T-shirts to my mix, someone selling DVDs could expand to selling DVD players or custom display cases for video collections.

The best part of starting a business out of a hobby is that it is self-motivating. Your interest alone in the subject will propel you to constantly brainstorm for new ways to expand. Would you believe that reading the sports section of the newspaper, visiting the Hockey Hall of Fame in Toronto, and even watching hockey games on TV contribute toward idea generation for expansion of my business? Well, they do—and I couldn't think of a better way to do business research than sitting back in a recliner with a drink and a bag of chips, watching Hockey Night in Canada! Now you can see why working on a hobby-based business doesn't seem like work at all, if you enjoy the subject area. Another benefit of enjoying doing research for your business is that it will never become stagnant, which is a common problem for many new ventures.

I enjoy what I do, and I hope I can develop it enough to pay the bills for many years to come. A business based on a hobby can be a satisfying career for anyone. Starting small and expanding as your marketplace knowledge grows is a great alternative for the reluctant first-time young entrepreneur. Can you think of a better job than one that entails your favorite pastime?

From Dreams to Reality: The Making of an Entrepreneur

Jennifer Nies
Aqua Clear Aquarium Services

Great Lakes Region
Regional Partner:
St. Cloud State University

Jennifer Nies

The past year has brought about many changes for both Aqua Clear Aquarium Service and Jennifer Nies. Since the Collegiate Entrepreneurs' Organization Conference in Washington, D.C., in November 2002, Jennifer participated in numerous public appearances, including panel discussions and presentations aimed at young entrepreneurs. In addition, she has been featured in numerous local and statewide newspapers and magazines for both her scholastic and entrepreneurial accomplishments. Because of all the publicity, Aqua Clear has grown by leaps and bounds. Aqua Clear is now planning to enter new markets and hire its first employees. Jennifer recently graduated summa cum laude from St. Cloud State University with a bachelor of science degree in communication studies with an emphasis in marketing and a minor in psychology. She plans to attend St. Cloud State University in the fall of 2003 to pursue a master of science degree in industrial-organizational psychology. Within the next five years, Jennifer aspires to earn a doctorate in industrial-organizational psychology and eventually teach at the college level. Regardless of her academic path, however, Jennifer will forever be involved in at least one entrepreneurial endeavor because, as she puts it, "Entrepreneurship is my passion!"

Aqua Clear Aquarium Service

FOUNDER:	Jennifer Nies
WEB:	aquaclear.com
EMAIL:	jenny@aquaclear.com
PHONE:	320/266-2108
ADDRESS:	1732 7th Street SE St. Cloud MN 56304

Are entrepreneurs born? Could it be that at birth certain babies have an entrepreneurial gene located somewhere in their little bodies that stimulates a hunger deep within them—a hunger to indulge in risk-taking endeavors throughout the course of their lives? Even though the obvious answer is no, it is interesting to imagine what the world would be like if entrepreneurial qualities could be implanted into a person's genetic makeup. But until this becomes a reality, the questions remain: If entrepreneurs are not born, then what makes someone an entrepreneur? And more importantly, what does it mean to be one? Unfortunately, there are no obvious or definite answers to these questions, but as a young female entrepreneur, I do have some insights into these inquiries.

Although entrepreneurship is not genetically engineered, I believe that there is something truly special about an entrepreneur. Some say it's luck; others say it's intuition. I say it is a person's ability to act on his or her ideas and to take wise risks, risks that set him or her apart to make a true entrepreneur. This assertion stems from my own experiences—I took action, I incurred risks, and I succeeded.

As co-owner of Aqua Clear Aquarium Service, an aquarium design, installation, and maintenance company located in St. Cloud, Minnesota, my story is distinctive. I begin with my very first business endeavor at the young age of eight, the lemonade stand.

While most kids were playing at the park or swimming at the local pool, I was planning and gathering my materials. Every summer I led my younger sister and cousins in an exciting business venture—the lemonade stand. Unlike most other lemonade stand operations, however, we differentiated our products and services. Whereas our competitors sold only one product, lemonade, we offered a plethora of what I now call junk, but back then our products were small treasures to our customers. We sold everything from the traditional lemonade to the adults to seashells and friendship bracelets to the kids in the neighborhood. We spent the off-season months, which were the fall, winter, and spring months, collecting and creating our goods to sell.

In addition to our product line, we also offered a credit card option to our clients. Here's how it worked: Those customers who absolutely had to have our products but did not have the means to pay for them at that particular time were offered a special deal. They could purchase a credit card for one dollar and take the merchandise home with them that day under one condition—they had to pay their balance, which was the sticker price of the product they had purchased with their credit card, within one week. One of the first lessons we learned at this early age was that not all people keep their word, and legal means were sometimes needed to collect payment; this included having an older brother or sister persuade our clients to pay their debt or else. . . .

So, how does a childhood pastime relate to the start-up of an aquarium business? Looking back now, our endeavors seem funny and entertaining, but they really taught me three very important lessons that have helped me to succeed today.

First of all, I learned that running a business takes a great deal of hard work and dedication. As a lemonade stand owner, I soon found out that I did not have the luxury of taking the day off to go to the park with my friends; I had responsibilities and obligations to fulfill to both my customers and employees.

Secondly, I learned that establishing a strong, positive relationship with customers and employees creates brand loyalty. Day after day and summer after summer, customers returned to my lemonade stand for service. Why? The answer is quite simple: I learned that if you treat people with the respect that they deserve and take the time to understand their needs, they will bring their business back in the future.

Lastly and most importantly, my childhood business venture helped me to transform my true passions into profits. Even at the young age of eight, I knew I was a people-person. I loved talking and working with people, and I was good at it. My dad once told me that I could sell the Pope a double bed or snow to the Eskimos. It was not until junior high that I discovered a second passion—animals, more specifically, aquatic animals. In the eighth grade, I received my first pair of guppies, a small breed of freshwater fish known for their beautiful and colorful tails. I cared for my guppies like they were my children. In fact, I cared too much; I ended up overfeeding them, killing them in the process. I was so devastated that I made a promise to myself that when I got new fish, I would care properly for them. From that day on, I read multiple aquatic books and articles and convinced my dad to set up an old twenty-gallon aquarium for me to put my new fish in. To me, that twenty-gallon was a masterpiece. A few years later, I was lucky enough to get a job at a local pet store to help support my new-found hobby. It was at this store that I met my business partner, Jim, and my very first client.

Jim and I met in 1996 at Crossroads Pet Center. I had worked there for a couple months before he was hired so when he came, I helped him get acquainted with the store. Over time, we became great friends and spent countless hours discussing dreams of opening our own pet store and cramming notebooks full of ideas and plans for what we considered to be an ideal retail operation. We even devised a list of potential names and logos for our pet shop. At the time, Jim was studying aquatic biology at St. Cloud State University, and I was still in high school. I was fascinated with his knowledge of aquatics, and he was intrigued by my ability to work with people. Together, we knew we would make a fabulous team.

In the winter of 1997, a woman came into the store, and all at once our dreams became reality. We took the risk—we acted. She wanted a salt-water aquarium but expressed concern about her lack of knowledge in the area. It was at that moment the light bulb went on. We had the knowledge and passion: We could set-up and maintain an aquarium for her. Jim had already dabbled in the field for a year or so under the Aqua Clear name, so he had some knowledge of starting and operating a business of this sort. That night, we met at his apartment after work and discussed the logistics of our business. The next morning we called our first client to set up a time to install her aquarium.

Since that day, Aqua Clear has expanded to six surrounding cities, offering a full range of aquarium services including the design, installation, and maintenance of aquariums for business offices and private homes. Aqua Clear also stocks a variety of aquarium essentials including tropical fish, marine fish, invertebrates, and a small range of dry goods.

Even though we still continue to grow and expand to new areas, Aqua Clear has not been without its problems. From a slumping economy and negligent clients to passionate disagreements between the two of us, Jim and I have traveled our share of rough roads and have overcome many obstacles over the years. But after battling all the tough times and celebrating the victories, if I could to do it over again, I would do two specific things differently.

First of all, I cannot emphasize enough the importance of writing out a formalized business plan. Without one, roles and responsibilities can and will become confused. For example, starting a business with a partner is somewhat like moving in with a new roommates in that rules need to be established before you settle in; otherwise paths gets crossed and people get irritated. Had Jim and I established our rules in the form of a business plan, we could have had something to fall back on when the rules were broken. Business plans do take time to develop; however, if I had known how much time creating a plan would have saved me in the long run, I would have put forth the effort in the very beginning to formally write out our goals and business objectives.

Secondly, as I now know, it is essential to understand the differences between the legal forms of business organization. When Aqua Clear Aquarium Service became a legal entity, we did not know the benefits and drawbacks connected with the different forms, namely the distinction between a general partnership and a limited partnership. For a business like Aqua Clear, a limited partnership made more sense for the simple fact that if there were to be a legal claim against us, our liabilities were only as deep as the business. In other words, under this form, our personal property and/or assets could not be taken from us in the case of a legal liability dispute, debt, or obligation. Fortunately, Jim and I have never encountered any liability claims; however, had I fully understood the difference in liability, we would have been established as a limited partnership from the start.

I end my story with the answers to the questions posed in the beginning: What makes an entrepreneur and what does it mean to be one? Throughout my adventures as a business owner, I stand firm when I say that entrepreneurs possess something special. I believe that you don't have to have a certain IQ score or have a particular educational background to be successful. You don't have to be rich or live in a specific city to thrive. You just have to possess an idea and have the ability to act on it. I assert that entrepreneurs, like myself, succeed because we take what we love and apply it to what we know. We don't just sit back and wait for opportunities to come to us; we seek them out, and whenever possible, we take a chance and incur the risks, turning our dreams into reality.

So, what can you do to inspire the entrepreneur within yourself? I suggest two things. First, take some time to formalize what you know. Be creative as you write out your passions and goals and the ways in which you intend to embark on them. Have fun yet be realistic with your objectives. Secondly, tell your family and friends about your aspirations and ask for their input. I discovered that advice and guidance from those you trust is truly priceless. Moreover, as you verbalize your ideas to others, you will gain the confidence and support needed for the transformation from dreams to reality.

There is Always a Way

Peter Stranathan

McGuyver Painting Specialists

High Plains Region
Regional Partner:
Benedictine College

Peter Stranathan

Peter recently graduated from Colorado State University with majors in entrepreneurship and marketing. McGuyver Painting was founded in 2000 and is owned and operated by Peter Stranathan and Jeremy Pourbaix. McGuyver Painting is a residential and commercial painting company operating in Fort Collins, Colorado. It remained small for two years, with Peter and Jeremy handling all aspects of its operation until 2002, when the company grew to ten employees. As McGuyver Painting expanded, it tackled several new markets. Currently, it employs about thirty people. Since its inception, McGuyver Painting has obtained one hundred percent customer satisfaction through a strong commitment to open communication and creative problem solving. The company slogan "There is Always a Way" exemplifies the way business is conducted in every aspect of McGuyver Painting. Ambitious dreams for the company's future and a strong track record of past accomplishments fuel the pride that swells in the hearts of its owners. The future is very promising for the young company as the owners continue expansion and hope to double sales each year for the next several years.

Peter has been exploring opportunities to participate within the community through outreach programs. Sponsorship of a community golf tournament for Push America and partnerships with low-income housing developments are currently under review. He now manages a store in Loveland, Colorado, and spends his free time expanding McGuyver Painting.

McGuyver Painting Specialists

FOUNDER: Peter Stranahan, Jeremy Pourbaix
WEB: mcguyverpainting.com
EMAIL: mcguyverpainting@hotmail.com
PHONE: 800/816-8651

T he character traits that make up the personality of an entrepreneur are often unique. Of course, no formula will allow you to create the perfect set of character traits in yourself to ensure that you will be successful in running your own business. The key is to discover what things you are good at, strive to become better at them, and put them into use doing something that makes you happy. McGuyver Painting got its start largely because of a character trait that was shared by both owners. That very important trait led to a belief. The belief shaped an experience, and a motto was established. The motto now encompasses our company's philosophies and culture. It is the driving force behind the success, growth, and passion in the business. Our motto is, "There is Always a Way." To better demonstrate this, let us tell you a story.

It was 10:30 P.M. on a dark and twisting mountain highway. Headlights streaming in the opposite direction kept Peter, who was behind the wheel of the 1985 Honda CRX, keenly attuned to his surroundings. Jeremy, the sole passenger, struggled to get comfortable in the seat next to Peter. The small car was packed with painting supplies because the two had just finished another marathon painting adventure in the mountain town of Frisco, Colorado. It was not out of the ordinary for them to have worked the ninety-plus hours they had in the last five days in order to complete the job. This one had taken every ounce of daylight on that Friday to finish. Unfazed by the long day, Peter and Jeremy had packed up and were headed to Denver to retrieve a vehicle capable of hauling the rest of their equipment from Frisco to their home in Fort Collins. The plan was to arrive in Denver by 11:30 P.M. and return to Frisco with a van by 1:00 A.M. If all went well, they would arrive home between 3 and 4 A.M. However, along the way, things took an unexpected turn.

A phone call interrupted the purr of the road beneath the car. Peter's girlfriend, Leslie, had called to see how his day had gone. Peter drove while he explained the plan he and Jeremy had devised. They would have to drive until the wee hours of the morning to complete the task at hand. He was looking forward to spending time with Leslie that weekend, and Jeremy was anxious to get back home to his wife, Kayt. Leslie and Kayt, like everyone else who knew Peter and Jeremy, had grown accustomed to expecting these crazy if not impossible schemes. They knew that the duo always followed through with what they dreamed up. Peter and Jeremy planned to drive all night to get home, and no one doubted they would do it.

KABAAAMM!!

"Whoa! What the heck was that?" Peter exclaimed. Something had just struck the bottom of the car and made a racket audible even to Leslie on the other end of the cell phone. Jeremy, a little shocked by the unusual noise, ran through a checklist of things for Peter to test to ensure the car was still operating correctly.

"Steering?" Jeremy asked.

"Seems fine," Peter responded.

"Accelerator?"

"We're good."

"Clutch?"

"Still there."

"Hmmm . . . and the radio is still working. I guess we're all right," said Jeremy.

"Okay, let's keep moving," Peter responded, becoming more at ease. "I have had this car for years, and it tends to make funny noises sometimes. Maybe something just flew up from the road." Peter returned to his phone conversation and some five minutes later, hung up with Leslie.

A bright orange sign in the distance broke up the monotonous streaking of the painted lane lines. It read CONSTRUCTION ZONE. Soon the road went from two lanes to one. As the cars ahead slowed, Peter tried to downshift. Immediately, he noticed something was wrong.

"OH MY GOSH! WE'VE GOT NOTHING! THE TRANSMISSION IS GONE!" Peter yelled as he grasped the transmission stick and twirled it in circles. There was no longer any way to shift gears. Something had happened under the car, rendering the transmission inoperable. With the construction cones on both sides of the narrow lane, there was no way to turn off, no exit to take, and no shoulder on which to safely pull off. Their only option was to try and coast to a safe destination.

Luckily, the mountain road was steep and kept the car coasting far longer than would have otherwise been possible. A few minutes passed, and the car was now gliding at just thirty miles an hour down the interstate. Just in time, they spotted a glimpse of hope. The sign ahead read END CONSTRUCTION ZONE. The road had flattened and the CRX was moving at less than fifteen mph. Peter took the first opportunity he had to pull off on the shoulder and stop the car.

As he exited the car, he said to Jeremy, "I'll look to see what's wrong."

"Sounds good," Jeremy replied and then asked, "Where is your car jack? I'll get the car in the air so that you can crawl under and check things out."

"I don't have a jack," Peter said.

The two retrieved a light from the trunk and plugged it in to the cigarette lighter. Relieved that it worked, they began to problem-solve. They needed to come up with a plan. Peter explained that he thought he knew what the problem was but would have to get further under the car to be sure. This would be their first obstacle.

First, Jeremy had to lift the car as high as he could, while Peter slid underneath. Then, Jeremy lowered the car over Peter's neck where there was an inch of clearance. This solution, although unorthodox, solved their initial problem. It was at this point that they both realized that they had stopped in a horrible place. Peter looked toward the back of the car as he heard traffic approaching. A semi-truck went by, and caused his heart to jump as it roared just feet from the car he was under.

"Oh man! We stopped right around a blind curve!" Peter exclaimed. Jeremy looked and regretfully agreed. The ninety-degree turn in the road just before their current position made it impossible for other drivers to see them until moments before they passed. With this danger in mind, the two hurried their efforts of repairing the car.

Peter was correct in his initial diagnosis of the problem; the transmission linkage had disconnected from the shifter and made it impossible to change gears. The bolt that held the two parts together had likely been the culprit of the loud noise some twenty minutes earlier. It was a relief to identify the problem; however, they did not have a bolt to replace the missing one. Additionally, the two pieces that needed to be aligned were exceptionally hard to reach. Getting home anytime soon would require these two entrepreneurs to accomplish the impossible.

Peter climbed back out from under the car. He and Jeremy started rummaging through the back of the car where all their painting supplies were kept. They needed something to replace the missing bolt. After discussing several possibilities, they found a drill bit set.

"Ah ha!" exclaimed Peter. "All we have to do is find the right size drill bit and put it where the bolt used to be!"

This seemed like a feasible tool to fill the void of the missing bolt. The car was so low that Peter had to attempt the fix without looking at what he was doing. After a few minutes of working blindly to insert the drill bit into the transmission linkage, Peter deemed it impossible and climbed out again from under the car to resume the search for a solution. He and Jeremy decided they needed some sort of string or wire to align the parts so that the drill bit could be inserted and held into position. With no rope, wire, or string anywhere to be found, the two were moments away from giving up.

But they had failed to look in one place: on themselves! Peter quickly removed a shoelace and asked Jeremy to once again lift the car. Peter fished the shoelace through the bolt holes to align the transmission linkage. He then pulled the shoelace tight and as expected, the holes aligned. Next, he inserted the drill bit. It slid right into place. Now all that was left to do was to secure the drill bit in place so that it would not fall out. Jeremy was one step ahead. He had already retrieved something every paint crew has on hand that would complete the job: masking tape. As he handed a roll under the car, Peter exclaimed, "Perfect!" He completed the repair by taping each end of the bit to hold it in place. Jeremy raised the car once more so that Peter could remove himself from beneath its chassis. They returned to their seats to find out if all of their efforts had paid off.

The car started right up, but would the MacGuyver-like fix hold as they attempted to put the car in gear? Peter pushed the clutch down and crossed his fingers. He pushed forward on the shifter. Something clicked as it went into gear. They had done it! As he fished for first gear, he realized that their fix had only given them third gear to work with. It was better than nothing.

Peter and Jeremy traveled nearly seventy more miles that

night in third gear. They were the slowest car on the road, but at least they were moving! An hour later, they were headed back up the mountain in the van. They would be home in a few short hours.

During this trip, they had a chance to comprehend what had just been accomplished. It was much more than just fixing a car. They realized that if they could do this, they possessed the ingenuity and determination to do anything they set their minds to. They discovered there is always a way!

That night taught Jeremy and Peter volumes about themselves and ultimately gave them the mindset they needed to start their own business. This discovery allowed them to see that there truly is always a way. This motto now applies to every situation in their lives and is the driving force behind McGuyver Painting.

If there is always a way, then it is only logical that you must do what it takes to accomplish your objective. When the car broke down on the side of the road in the middle of the night, Peter and Jeremy took action. They relied on each other for help. They used their resources at hand to solve their problem. They overcame all of the obstacles in their way and accomplished their objective. It was an unexpected challenge, but they did what it took to get the job done . . . no matter how late it was, what dangers stood in the way, or how tired they were.

As the car rolled to a stop on the side of the highway, they knew they would do what it took to fix the car. As they stepped out of the car, they immediately began a problem-solving process. The one bolt that they really needed was many miles behind them, somewhere on the side of the highway. They only had a few items with them in the car. If they were going to fix this on their own, it would mean accomplishing the impossible. They found a creative solution with what they had to solve the problem. Their ingenuity led them ultimately to fix a transmission with a drill bit, a shoelace, and some masking tape.

It took more than a belief that there is always a way and the ability to problem-solve to get their car back on the road. It also took a tremendous amount of teamwork. Teamwork is very important in any business. Not only is it important to be willing to work on a team, it is also essential to surround yourself with quality individuals on your team. As Jeremy and Peter pushed through adversity and utilized problem-solving techniques that night, they made a great team. They could accomplish more than twice as much working as a team than either one of them could have on their own.

Today, they do what it takes to solve problems that are often larger than that night on the side of the road. They have been faced with how to control cash flow in a rapidly growing company. They have battled through issues of corporate culture and have been challenged to teach others how to run their businesses successfully. These challenges that they face now demand creative solutions, ingenuity, and at times accomplishing what seems to be the impossible.

Chances are, you see a little of yourself in the story of Jeremy and Peter. Possibly, you have started identifying your own character traits as you read about theirs. It is extremely important to discover and develop your strongest character traits. These traits are what will shape your beliefs and influence your actions throughout your entire life. Identifying them and developing them early is important so that you can use them to their fullest potential in your life and in your business. Nurturing and building upon your strongest traits will make you more effective because you can intentionally utilize them in every situation. As college students recognize their strengths, they choose specific areas of study that encourage them to train for a job they'll enjoy. You need to find your strengths and build upon them in order to build a business and a life that you will enjoy and succeed in.

By defining and nurturing your strongest character traits, you can develop a motto that will help you put your character traits into action. Eventually, that motto will become more than just a good slogan; it will define your company. At McGuyver Painting, "There is Always a Way" means persistence, determination, and ingenuity. What do your character traits mean to you? This is your motto! How will you utilize this in your daily life and in your business?

If you have the drive of an entrepreneur, then there is no doubt that you will quickly identify the assets that you have in yourself. Build on these traits and utilize them to your fullest ability. You have in front of you a great opportunity. You have the chance to be successful, to help others succeed, and to do what really makes you happy. Good luck!

Global Student Entrepreneur Awards

The Global Student Entrepreneur[SM] Awards recognize those outstanding undergraduate student entrepreneurs who are simultaneously juggling course work and cash flows—and succeeding at both!

Finalists must produce more than just a financially successful business. Their company's quality, service, adaptation to change, and social impact are evaluated by an international panel of judges.

To apply for the award or to obtain further information, please visit www.gsea.org.

Instruction Manual Available
to Teachers of Entrepreneurship

This book can be used as a text
for middle school, high school
or college students
interested in entrepreneurship.

To receive a copy,
send your request to gsea@slu.edu.
The manual will be emailed to you.

Notes

∞

Notes

Notes

∞

Notes
∞

Notes

∞

Notes
∞

Notes

∞

Notes

Notes
∞

Notes
∞